VECTORS TO SPARE

Vectors

THE LIFE OF AN

to Spare

AIR TRAFFIC CONTROLLER

Milovan S. Brenlove

Iowa State University Press / Ames

Milovan Brenlove is assistant professor of aviation at Daniel Webster College in Nashua, New Hampshire. He is a longtime pilot, an active flight instructor, and an experienced aviation writer. His primary interest, based on twelve years of experience as an air traffic controller, is improving the relationship between pilots and controllers. Brenlove is the author of *The Air Traffic System: A Commonsense Guide*.

© 1993 Iowa State University Press, Ames, Iowa 50010

⊗ Printed on acid-free paper in the United States of America

First edition, 1993

Library of Congress Cataloging-in-Publication Data

Brenlove, Milovan S.
    Vectors to spare: the life of an air traffic controller / Milovan S. Brenlove.—1st ed.
        p.   cm.
    ISBN 0-8138-0471-X (alk. paper)
    1. Air traffic controllers. 2. Air traffic control—Vocational guidance.
I. Title.
TL725.3.T7B666   1993
629.136′6′092—dc20   92-45892

To the memory of my father, R. Rhody Brenlove,

whose unconditional love guided me in ways

I may never fully realize, and to my mother,

Diana V. Brenlove, whose unfailing love and

belief in me gave me the spirit to keep trying

It always seemed as though a controller's well-worn, familiar, comfortable headset would break right in the midst of a heavy traffic session. Attributing much of his or her success to that small inanimate object, more than one controller has been heard to remark, **"I hate to give up a headset that still has good vectors to spare left in it."**

CONTENTS

PREFACE

IT HAS BEEN SEVERAL YEARS SINCE I LAST VECTORED AN AIRPLANE to the final at Greater Pittsburgh International Airport, or stood in the newest and tallest FAA-owned tower in the country trying to figure out which airplane was which as I gazed almost two miles away to the terminal building. In 1987 I finally ended my on-again, off-again relationship with the Federal Aviation Administration, a career that spanned a sometimes rocky fifteen years.

For almost that long I have wanted to write a book describing what it is really like to be an air traffic controller, to be a member of a profession that has suffered drastic changes over the past few years only to emerge essentially unchanged. The problem has been to sort out the events and the people in a manner that conveys a true sense of what it is like to perform a job most normal people either could not or would not care to do.

Air traffic controllers are, on the one hand, intelligent, articulate, and courageous individuals performing a difficult task under conditions that are seldom ideal. They are, on the other hand, irreverent, comical, and extremely independent misfits who somehow always seem to get the job done in spite of themselves and endless reams of bureaucratic regulations. I wanted to get down on paper the uniqueness of these people and the pride I felt in sharing part of my life with them.

After dozens of rewrites, the answer seems to be that trying to pick and choose only the best examples and arrange their stories in proper order is unnecessary. The truth is that, while we controllers usually see ourselves as a special breed performing Herculean tasks on a daily basis, we are, or in my case were, just ordinary people working a slightly out-of-the-ordinary job. In any case, what follows is my history of the people I knew and the events that occurred—simply those times, those people, and those memories that keep coming back to me, as daydreams or nightmares. It is also an inside look at what being an air traffic controller meant.

Like any other specialized occupation, aviation has developed specialized practices and terminology that may need a little explaining. For example, pilots and controllers use something called the phonetic alphabet to represent each letter of the alphabet—Alpha for *A*, Bravo for *B*, Charlie for *C*, etc. This alphabet ensures that airplane callsigns (the numbers and letters used to identify each individual aircraft) won't be misunderstood in radio transmissions. Additionally, for clarity, controllers and pilots almost always say each number used in a clearance separately—two two three instead of two twenty-three. The now-old-fashioned clock face is also an important code. "Traffic at twelve o'clock" tells the pilot there's another airplane straight ahead. Three o'clock means it's on the pilot's right, and one or two o'clock means it's somewhere in-between. The glossary should clarify other aviation terms and phrases. If something is still unclear, just ask your favorite pilot or call your local flight school. Most people connected with flying like to talk about it and will be glad to help you out.

So what is it really like to be an air traffic controller? On a good day it's like being the mastermind behind the game plan of the victors on Superbowl Sunday. On a bad day it's more like being a banjo player sitting in the middle of the New York Philharmonic. But whether the days were good or bad, for twelve years I would not have wanted to be anywhere else. And now, having said my good-byes to the special band of individuals who inhabit those monolithic tributes to bureaucratic barrenness, I have enough memories to keep me satisfied for a long time to come.

Pilots who read this book will note that the camaraderie between controllers bears a strong resemblance to that among aviators. They will understand the lighthearted approaches to impending crises as legitimate defense mechanisms. Passengers who reluctantly relinquish their fates to the civil servants on the ground should remember the "Big Sky" theory by which most controllers live: No matter how much you screw up, it's hard as hell to run two airplanes together.

ACKNOWLEDGMENTS

Although I mention only a few pilots and controllers in this book, I would like to thank the many thousands more for whom it has been written. However brief our time together may have been, each of those people I came to know added to the joy I experienced as an air traffic controller.

To the people at Iowa State University Press, and in particular to Bill Silag and Jane Zaring, thank for the belief in and support of a project that has been a dream of mine for many years.

Finally, to Mary Russell Curran, an editor for who I have gained the greatest respect and admiration, thank for your tireless efforts in helping to make this book the best it could possibly be.

VECTORS TO SPARE

TOO CLOSE TO CALL

I VIVIDLY REMEMBER SITTING IN JIM'S BIG OF-
FICE IN TOLEDO, OHIO, plush by government standards, not bad by anyone else's. With me were my
wife and our one-year-old daughter, all three making our first visit to the airport that would be my
office for at least the next several years, we hoped.

This was not my first experience in the world of air traffic
control. Twelve months before meeting Jim I had walked into the
radar room at Akron-Canton Regional Airport and for the very
first time viewed the inner sanctum, the very nerve center of the
airport, and thought to myself, what the hell am I doing here? Six
months later I had walked out of there vowing never to return to
that crazy crew known to most as the animals.

During my brief but rather comprehensive indoctrination into
the ways of the FAA, I had seen the beginning of the militancy
that seven years later would culminate in the firing of more than
eleven thousand controllers; had witnessed my first airliner crash;
had begun an after-work ritual of drinking to excess with the rest
of my crew; and had had my one and only trip to the FAA
Training Academy in Oklahoma City cancelled because of the fuel
crisis. By the end of that first six months I didn't know a lot about
air traffic control, but I did know that unless I wanted my young
marriage to end suddenly, and unless I wanted to watch my health

and sanity slip right out from under me, I had to get out of the
FAA. What I didn't realize was that I had already become addicted
to the excitement and the challenge. In spite of everything, I liked,
or more accurately loved, being an air traffic controller.

So in the fall of 1974, having been careful not to burn any
bridges behind me, I conned my wife and the FAA into giving me
one more chance. With my official confirmation telegram in hand,
I moved my family and our meager belongings into a Toledo
townhouse that, not unlike me, was just bouncing back from
bankruptcy to give life another go.

Jim was the tower chief, the chief controller at Toledo
Express Airport. He welcomed my family and me into his office
and said, "There's been a mistake. We aren't to accept any more
controller trainees in Toledo. You were supposed to be assigned
to Mansfield Tower, in the central part of the state." As if the
marathon of packing all our belongings into the rental truck,
driving over two hundred miles, and setting up house in a town we
knew only from the familiar sacred expression weren't enough,
Mansfield Tower was a nonradar approach control facility out in
the middle of nowhere. The look of total exasperation on my
mate's face echoed my thoughts of almost a year earlier. What the
hell are we doing here?

Whether or not our signed lease and our already unloaded
furniture constituted a legal obligation for the FAA to move us to
Mansfield, Ohio, never became an issue. Out of the goodness of
their hearts, the FAA and Jim decided to let me stay in Toledo to
see if I had what it took to become not only an air traffic controller but a radar controller as well.

Jim had one more thing to say to me that day, and only after
many years as a faithful civil servant in aviation did I begin to
understand the wisdom of his words. He wished me well, told me
his door was always open, and said I had the full support of
everyone at Toledo. He also told me to remember one thing: if I
wanted to climb the ladder of success in the FAA I should move
on and up from each facility or position before my shining star
became tarnished. Unfortunately, in the years that followed I
carried a worn little star and no silver polish, yet somehow I always
seemed to have help when I needed it most. Help first arrived in
the person of Al Schwitz, operating initials AN.

For some reason, regardless of how hard I try to conjure up

a more fitting comparison, Al's physical appearance brings to mind a possum. I don't know why that is, because I'm not even sure exactly what a possum looks like. I've no doubt, though, that if a possum were describing himself to a rabbit he would say, "I look like an Al Schwitz." Al was a compound anomaly. His long, pointed nose, his thinning hair, his graying mustache, his meticulously maintained suit, and his broad, enthusiastic smile could have made most outsiders mistake him for almost anything but what he was. But the first instant in which you made personal contact with Al, all that changed. The gentleman was a professional who completely and continuously loved his job and the people who worked for him. In the year that I worked for and with Al I learned not only how to become an air traffic controller but also what kind of a controller I wanted to be.

Al came to us after working in the Indianapolis Tower, and every now and then he brought a little of it with him. Once a year, on the Memorial Day weekend, the busy but orderly airspace that surrounds Indianapolis airport becomes saturated with hundreds upon hundreds of pilots flying in to see the Indy 500. And if the weather happens to be good, the traffic gets even heavier. Al always called good-weather days great race days.

As we went to work in Toledo that cloudless Sunday afternoon for the three-to-eleven shift, we all knew what was in store for us when Al looked out the window, rubbed his hands together, and gleefully announced, "What a great day for the race!" Every pilot and budding pilot within fifty miles of Toledo would be out there "building time," adding precious hours to his or her logbook.

Unlike controllers at the major metropolitan airports, who look forward to the weekends' reduced airline schedules as a respite from the hectic pace of the business week, controllers at small- and medium-sized airports frequently view them as their ultimate challenge. A Saturday of fair weather will usually increase the traffic count by at least 200 airplanes. A whole weekend of exceptionally good weather, particularly if it follows a spell of bad weather, can easily increase the controllers' workload by 1,000 planes. Of those 1,000 pilots, around 250 will have a "valuable learning experience." Consequently, many of the controllers on duty will find their own horizons significantly expanded.

Having recently completed my training and received a

checkout on local control, I was ready—barely—to take the position pilots refer to as Toledo Tower. I was in charge of safely and efficiently separating all arriving and departing airplanes within the immediate vicinity of the airport.

When most people think of air traffic controllers, they picture them in that highly visible, glass-encased room atop either the terminal building or some other prominent airport structure. For controllers, that tower cab with the panoramic view is really just the tip of the iceberg. Hidden somewhere underneath that room is the TRACON (terminal radar approach control), more commonly called the radar room.

At all but a few airports, like Chicago's O'Hare, controllers work in both the tower and the radar room. Although seldom seen by the general public, that dark, windowless radar room filled with the faint glow from as many as a dozen radarscopes is where the real challenge lies. Tower controllers are responsible only for the traffic they see in the area immediately around the airport; TRACON controllers have much broader responsibilities.

Through a combination of communications procedures and radar information presented as little blips on their scopes, controllers in the TRACON are responsible for all the traffic within a thirty- or forty-mile radius of the airport. Any pilot inbound to or outbound from the main airport must communicate with at least one of those controllers. At any given time, the men and women in the radar room can collectively be responsible for as many as fifty to seventy-five airplanes.

To me, the tower seemed bewildering enough, and I knew my work as a controller-in-training had just begun. With my official government-issue sunglasses firmly attached to my headset, I plugged my umbilical cord into the console that for the next hour or so would connect me to every pilot within hearing range of the airport. Having heard all the tales of horror told by the veterans, I was about to start making a list of my own. Almost immediately I experienced what became my first "You shoulda seen what happened" story.

Because of the heavy traffic that day, our normal one-runway operation was expanded to include runway 34—which we always say as "three four"—for overflow arrivals and departures. This made my job more difficult, because runway 34 crossed runway 7, our main runway, at a point that allowed only 4,425 feet of runway

34 to be used without infringing on runway 7. Certain larger
airplanes could not land on runway 34 and hold short (remain
clear) of runway 7 when other planes were simultaneously landing
on runway 7. Despite that potential difficulty, I was "movin' some
tin" and having a good time getting airplanes into and out of the
airport using the minimum legal requirements as set forth by the
FAA.

Then through my headset came the voice of a crewmember
from down in the radar room. A locally based Grumman Gulfstream executive airplane was inbound for runway 34 and said he
could hold short of runway 7 with no problem. He would most
likely land on runway 34 the same time, or very nearly so, that a
flight of four F-100 military fighters would be arriving on runway
7. Would I buy the deal? I too readily agreed to work it out.

Two reasons prompted my decision. Everyone knew that
radar was where the real action was, and when radar called up and
said they wanted something, you gave it to them. Having spent only
a few sessions in the radar room just to observe, I was in no
position to dispute what seemed a valid request. The other reason
was that this pilot, as many pilots are prone to do on their home
turf, could become irate when controllers didn't give him the
service he deserved. If he said he could land and stop his airplane
in less than 4,425 feet, I wasn't going to be the one to tell him
otherwise.

As the situation developed I did my thing, cool and professional. When the Gulfstream pilot reported on a four-mile final for
runway 34, I said, "Grumman nine hundred, cleared to land
runway three four. Hold short of runway seven. Traffic a flight of
four F-100s landing runway seven."

The F-100s, still about eight miles from the airport, checked
in for an overhead approach. The overhead meant that the flight
of four fighters would come screaming into the airport at speeds
in excess of three hundred knots, and when directly over the
runway they would split up and fly in a tight pattern to the runway,
landing one right after another no more than a few seconds apart.
It also meant that if the Gulfstream decided at the last minute that
he could not remain clear of runway 7, well then, if the first F-100
didn't get him there were three others waiting in line to take a
shot.

As the first F-100 approached on short final, I gave him the good news. "Bison one one (the official, if rather ludicrous, military callsign), traffic is a Gulfstream, landing runway three four. Will hold short of your runway."

His reply, "I certainly hope so." The F-100, after all, was an aging fighter plane from the Korean War era that had undergone several modifications over its lifetime, all of which added substantial weight. That meant that every landing required a drag parachute, hot brakes, and every bit of the ten-thousand-foot runway. If any airplane had to stop in a hurry, it was clear that it wasn't going to be one of the F-100s.

My eyes began wildly scanning first one runway, then the other, and then back again. It became obvious to everyone in the tower that what I had going was a DAT, a dead-ass tie, a tight situation controllers frequently describe with this saying: "In the event of a tie, duplicate prizes will most likely NOT be awarded." As I felt the knot in my stomach tighten and grow, I knew that all I could do was watch and hope for the safe resolution of a bad decision.

By the time I realized I should have sent the Gulfstream around—instructed him not to land but to overfly the runway at a safe altitude—he was inches above the runway. Most likely, he couldn't begin a go-around at that point and still gain enough altitude to safely fly over the F-100s rolling out on runway 7. So I continued to do all that I could—watch. My heart pounded louder and louder and my legs became weaker and weaker. I began to sweat as I had never sweated before.

The Gulfstream rolled closer to the intersection and grew larger in size than I had ever imagined possible. All other activity in the tower stopped as three sets of eyes watched and waited. Then the plane finally stopped about a hundred feet short of the intersection where the two runways met. One by one, the four F-100s rolled past the Gulfstream, each cautiously sliding over to the cold side of the runway.

Even before I could give thanks to the sky above, Al came bounding up the tower steps two at a time. "That operation didn't look too good on the scope downstairs. How'd it look from up here?"

"Worse!" is what I recall saying.

He went on to tell me what I already knew: besides being illegal, it wasn't a very smart thing to do. I agreed.

"That won't happen again, will it?" he asked. I said no. Then Al gave me a fatherly pat on the back. "Enough said," and he went back down to the radar room.

By every measure in the book he could have, and maybe should have, done a whole lot more. Although the radar controller had handed me what I later thought was a poor situation to begin with, I had the opportunity and the responsibility to cancel his decision. Instead I foolishly carried it through to its conclusion, allowing a system error. Had the Gulfstream pilot already touched down on runway 34 and then said he could stop short of runway 7, I would have been legal and wise. But because runway 34 wasn't long enough and the pilot had given me his reassurance while still in the air, my decision was wrong.

National headquarters in Washington could have been alerted to send out their "go team," and I could immediately have been pulled off the position pending an investigation. Today, pilots and controllers are forced to dish out punishment instead of seeking solutions to system problems. Al, however, felt this new controller had somehow learned his lesson. No one had been injured, and to carry it further would have done more harm than good. Whatever he saw in me that I didn't see in myself, he was right. In the years that followed I made more than one or two approach controllers mad when they got back airplanes that simply wouldn't fit where they wanted them to, but I never again put other people's lives in danger trying to make a bad situation work.

I like to think it was Al's sticking his neck out for me that made me do the same thing for another controller several years later. By then I was a full-fledged radar controller, working Arrival South on a busy day of heavier-than-usual traffic and less-than-ideal weather. I had accepted a handoff on a particular aircraft, N512PC, from a controller in Cleveland Center—the air traffic facility responsible for the airspace between airports—with control to turn or descend Papa Charlie at my discretion. I descended the pilot of Papa Charlie to 7,000 feet and told him about unknown traffic at one o'clock, four miles northwestbound, fully expecting him not to see an airplane that I assumed would be at a higher altitude in Cleveland Center's airspace.

The pilot responded that he had the traffic in sight and estimated the plane to be at around 7,500 feet. The weather was not at all conducive to pilots' flying in visual conditions, and I decided to ask someone to look into the situation. It turned out that a busy controller at Cleveland Center had forgotten to pass along to me for my control an airplane on an instrument flight plan flying in Toledo's airspace. Before I could get N512PC turned away from the other aircraft, the required three-mile separation had deteriorated to a mile or two. A system error had again occurred.

It was up to me. If I were to tell what really happened, Washington would be notified in a matter of minutes and an investigation initiated. If I were to stretch the truth, the matter of why that airplane was allowed to invade my airspace unannounced would still have to be investigated, but it would then be resolved more informally at the local level. As I thought about it, my anger at being innocently dragged into a possible midair collision gave way to thoughts of my own mistake a few years earlier.

Although I had never met that particular controller from Cleveland Center, I knew who he was from his voice and his operating initials. Over time, controllers from one facility talk frequently to controllers from adjacent areas on lines called the interphone or landlines. By means of this complex and sometimes temperamental system of voice communications, thousands of bits of control information are passed. With that information comes a very real and accurate sense of who the people are at the other end of the line. Through the years strong friendships are formed with voices that are usually never matched to faces.

So it was with this "voice." On sight, I couldn't have picked him out of a crowd of two, but if I needed help to get me out of a jam with my traffic, I could count on him to say yes. I had my answer. Separation between N512PC and N4004L had never fallen below the required three miles; there was no system error.

Not long after my own "valuable learning experience" in the Toledo Tower, Al returned to Indianapolis. Personal matters made him give up a promotion at Toledo and go home. Then, as now, the FAA frowned on anyone who would put familial concerns ahead of promotional opportunities, but Al's priorities never wavered. I suspect he never reached his full potential in the FAA because of his decision, but I also suspect he always knew he had made the right one.

All in all, Al's return to Indianapolis left an emptiness in Toledo that took a long time to fill. He had taught us a lot more than just how to be good controllers. Sitting under the glass on my desk is a piece of paper on which is written Al's most famous saying: "Don't never, never, never, NEVER give up! AN, Toledo Tower."

AIRPORT 33

AT ONE TIME OR ANOTHER, EVERY AIR TRAF-
FIC CONTROLLER on the way to work feels it—the
very real stress of anticipating what the coming
shift will be like. To each controller, a different set
of circumstances means a different reaction to
what lies ahead.

To the radar controller, solid instrument weather means
hours of being totally responsible for each and every aircraft on the
frequency since pilots will be unable to use visual separation
methods. To the tower controller, the same weather usually means
the job will be easier, slower, and more methodical than it might
be on a bright sunny day. To almost every controller, the day of
the week plays a large role in determining what kind of a shift it
will be. Thursday from three to eleven will be a back breaker at
the big airports. Sunday at the same time will make the off-the-
beaten-path controllers earn their money. Big airport or small,
when controllers are busy with eight or ten airplanes, they are just
plain busy, and thinking about the prospects ahead of time doesn't
help.

Maybe that's why we were so caught off guard. As the three
of us went upstairs to take control of the Toledo Tower for the
rest of the afternoon and evening shift, the hazy summer sky and
the three- to five-miles visibility that made finding all but the

largest airliners a full-time task had long since been replaced by a bright, clear autumn afternoon.

As the day wore on, two or three fortunate pilots would enjoy the opportunity to experience flying at its very best, but most would just go home after another long day of work. I would spend the afternoon taking in the scenery while leisurely talking to the few pilots who trickled into or out of the airport, and I would get paid a respectable salary for doing it.

Only the tower console reminded me that I was enjoying the view while working. To the uninitiated, the array of dials, lights, and switches embedded in inclined metal panels that run the entire length of the tower just below the window ledge seemed to resemble the control room of the Starship *Enterprise*. But to those of us who called the tower our office, all that strange equipment translated into the tools of our trade. The radio frequency selection switches, the weather instruments, the airport lighting panel for runway and taxiway lights, the intercom lines, and the computer printout machine were just a small part of the massive equipment complex that kept us in business.

During busy traffic periods, the desklike extension attached to the bottom of the slanted console served as the work area. It housed the hundreds of paper flight strips, the notepads, the binoculars, and all the seemingly trivial memos that kept controllers and pilots working in harmony. During the more relaxed times of the day, the desk served an even more important function; it gave everyone in the tower a comfortable place upon which to rest their feet. As I repositioned myself to take full advantage of the console, I reveled in the thought that the pleasure of the moment would likely continue through the rest of the shift.

Even the returning F-100s, which routinely flew at speeds three to four times faster than the average light plane could muster, didn't seem to portend any unusual problems for handling the rest of the traffic. Having once learned that a Cessna only a mile or two away could not land and clear the runway in time for four F-100s still eight or nine miles away to use it, I was not about to repeat my mistake. The pilots in slower planes would have to patiently wait their turns.

Besides, I was working ground control when the two-place trainer version of the F-100 returned to the airport for a couple of practice instrument approaches. Most often all I had to say was,

"Roger, taxi to the ramp" or "Roger, taxi to runway seven." Either way, no one could accuse me of being under too much stress. When the call from downstairs came over the speaker at local control's position, I left my feet comfortably up on the console where they belonged.

"Get ready, the Hogs are comin' back. Bison two three, a single ship, wants a couple of ILS [instrument landing system] approaches." Somewhere along the line the F-100s had affectionately earned the nickname Hogs. Some said it was because they were fuel hogs, burning more aviation fuel in one hour than most general aviation planes would burn in a year. Others said it was because they were speed or runway hogs, using up enormous amounts of airspace and concrete every time they took to the skies. By the time I arrived at Toledo, whoever had come up with the nickname was long since gone, as was the truth behind the story.

Bison 23, however, would be less of a problem than usual. A single F-100 shooting an instrument approach would be much like any other aircraft inbound to the airport. The pilot would slow the airplane to a more normal 190 or 200 knots and slow even more when he moved closer to the runway in preparation for a landing. Except, of course, that a practice approach wouldn't culminate in a landing. To continue inbound and land would only create unnecessary wear on the airplane. Instead, the practice maneuver would end in a low approach, two or three hundred feet above the runway, with afterburner belching fire and smoke as the F-100 shot past the tower at eye level, literally shaking everything in its path, including the tower windows. Although few would admit it, even the most hardened and cynical controllers enjoyed the little airshow.

Bison 23 checked in with the tower and was cleared for a low approach. Both the controller working local and I started looking for the F-100, and at about a three- or four-mile final, we finally picked it up. We watched and waited for the pilot's report of a missed approach, the signal that he was done with this approach and ready to go out for another try. At about a half-mile final, we saw the telltale smoke indicating that the afterburner, the part of a jet engine that reburns a portion of the unspent fuel-air exhaust mixture and turns it into additional thrust, had been lit and he was about to "go miss." Then instantly everything went from normal to chaotic.

The nose of the F-100 pitched up to a higher-than-normal attitude and the aircraft began to perform the Sabre Dance, a term we later learned stemmed from the F-100's official name, the Super Sabre. The plane rolled to the right, then to the left and back to the right, as if eerily dancing on its tail. The second time it rolled to the right there was no recovery. Instead, the F-100 and its two occupants disappeared behind a row of trees on the south side of runway 7. The double-paned glass windows in the tower insulated us from the sound, but moments later a huge black cloud of smoke appeared in place of the missing jet.

In the tower we looked at each other, frozen in disbelief. Without a warning from either pilot, Bison 23 had crashed. Although neither of us knew whether parachutes could be used at an altitude of only three or four hundred feet, we looked in the sky for signs of a successful ejection, but there were none. As quickly as we stopped doing anything, we started doing everything.

My friend working local control hit the crash siren and called down to tell the controllers in the radar room what had happened. The airport needed to be closed immediately to avoid hindering the rescue equipment in the efforts to get to the downed fighter. We both wanted someone more experienced in these situations up in the tower with us, but before help could arrive, we had things to do. It seemed unlikely that anyone could have survived, but we had to try everything possible to help.

I quickly dialed into the airport terminal public address system and twice announced "Airport thirty-three," the code words that would alert only those needing to know that an accident had occurred. I then picked up the red crash phone sitting on the window ledge and waited for the four or five needed stations around the airport to respond. One by one they checked in, just as we did in our daily rehearsal of the procedure. Airport security, fire station, county office, Guard operations, and so on until the phone chain was completed. The exact words I used still remain clear in my mind: "We just lost an F-100. He went down south of the approach end of runway seven!"

Minutes later they started rolling out of the firehouse. Chief 1 would be in charge of the rescue efforts. Then, one after another, the crash trucks with the odd names followed, each one contacting ground control for clearance down or across the runway to the rising smoke. First came Big Walter, a huge, yellow twin diesel truck that carried thousands of gallons of light water, a special mixture designed to smother the intense fire of aviation fuel, all of which could be dispersed in a matter of a few minutes. Then came Purple K, named for reasons I cannot remember, followed by the rescue vehicles operated by the National Guard unit at the far end of the field. The Guard drivers had a more immediate sense of urgency, since they all knew it was one of their own that went down. Less than two or three minutes after the crash, ground control was a clutter of questions with few answers.

By then Al was in the tower, offering support and trying to find out what had happened. Were we at all involved with the accident? Or more specifically, did we do anything that caused the F-100 to suddenly have to go around? The answer was no. Al then reconfirmed for the controllers down in the radar room that no traffic would be accepted on either runway until the rescue trucks no longer needed them. I continued to direct each truck to the site as best I could. It turned out the crash had occurred not on airport property but across a two-lane highway in a field a little farther south. What I thought was the quickest way to the burning jet caused one truck to get bogged down in mud and several others to take longer than might have been necessary to reach the site. I could not have known this ahead of time, but the error nevertheless made me question my judgment later.

Those first ten or fifteen minutes after the crash were filled with all kinds of emotions. Two healthy active people instantly had their lives and the lives of all those who knew them changed forever. Before we had time to react, or even knew what we were supposed to react to, there was a call from the security phone at the bottom of the tower stairs. One of the local TV news teams had received word of the accident and wanted to come up and talk to us. Could we find time for them? Thankfully, in a rare display of anger, Al sent them away. There was still work to do and a certain amount of emotional shock to contend with.

About twenty minutes later, word finally came from the rescue team. One pilot, the base commander, had died instantly. The other pilot, the safety officer, was in critical condition with severe burns, and his survival was still very questionable. The controller working local and I were finally relieved from our positions to listen to the tape recording of the conversations before and after the accident and to write our statements. The official investigation had already begun, leaving us little time to reflect on what had happened before our eyes.

During the next few weeks, questions and interviews became as much a part of our daily routine as talking to pilots. At one point we were asked to attend a fact-finding conference at the Air National Guard base, not an attempt to find fault with anyone but rather an effort to learn exactly what had caused the crash. Although it seemed impossible we would be implicated as having contributed to the crash, stranger things had happened.

Throughout the entire investigative process, we never for a moment lacked Al's full support. After he listened to the tapes, he reassured us that we had acted both as professionally and as efficiently as possible. The fatality that resulted could not have been prevented no matter what we might have done or tried to do. Though the safety officer would spend the next few months in a burn center recovering from his injuries, the fact that he was alive at all was a tribute to everyone who responded to the accident. It was time to get back to traffic as usual.

The preliminary conclusions of the investigation were that, for whatever unknown reason, a mechanical failure or a dozen other possible causes, the pilots failed to keep the airplane at the correct speed and attitude necessary to keep it flying. They let it get too slow on final approach to the runway. At very low altitude, the most frequent result is the Sabre Dance, followed by complete loss of control. It all happened with such incredible speed that ejecting simply wasn't an option. This time the controllers had nothing to do with the accident, findings reassuring for us. But for a long time after the accident, whenever an F-100 made its approach to the runway, the memories and a tightness in the stomach returned until each aircraft was safely on the ground. The crash of Bison 23 may have just been one of those things, but it was one that most of us couldn't forget.

PILOT ERROR

THERE WERE, OF COURSE, LIGHTER MOMENTS IN THE TOWER, even if they didn't always start out that way. Having a penchant for being in the wrong place at the right time, I was working Toledo local control once again when the voice from the radar room intercom interrupted my thoughts. A local pilot returning from an early morning trip with his company's executive corps was inbound from the southwest and had just requested priority handling for his approach to the airport.

Priority handling is one of those semantic games pilots who might be in trouble have to play because of the legal implications that could follow. Were a pilot to declare an emergency when, in actuality, the situation turned out to be not exactly an emergency but kind of like one only different, and another pilot hurrying to get out of the way somehow ended up in trouble, the pilot declaring the emergency would most likely be in the midst of a real problem, a legal one.

The pilot of the twin-engine Rockwell Commander was letting us know that something was wrong but he evidently had it under control, for now. How long he could hold it together was another matter, and for reasons we didn't know, that wasn't a lot longer. Because of the winds, the active runway at Toledo that day was runway 25. We were landing all our traffic to the southwest. To use the designated runway, the Commander pilot would have to fly an extra three or four miles past the airport before he could turn around and land into the wind. This would add an extra few minutes to the flight. Apparently, the added distance or additional time was a concern the pilot and his passengers either couldn't or didn't want to face.

On initial contact with approach control, the pilot had stated that he had to land straight in on runway 7, opposite the direction of normal traffic flow. He could not accept any delay and he would not, under any circumstances, go around. Most pilots, and this pilot in particular, are usually not so adamant in their demands of air traffic controllers, however much they would like to be. Known for his quiet, easygoing attitude, over the years he'd never tried to disrupt normal events just to save himself or his passengers some time.

As that familiar knot imperceptibly began to take shape, I quickly tried to sort out the information I had at hand. Among corporate aircraft, there isn't a more reliable or rugged airplane than a Commander. Even with one engine shut down, the pilot should have no great difficulty landing, and although this airplane was being flown without the aid of a copilot, the pilot was known to be very capable. The possibility of an in-flight fire came to mind, but his insistence that emergency equipment not be called out seemed to rule that out. Almost as quickly, I ruled out sickness, injury, or carbon monoxide poisoning, any one of which would have necessitated medical assistance from the rescue squad. Nothing was making much sense, and that only added to my nervous anticipation.

Though it would be only a few minutes before the pilot landed his troubled airplane, waiting was still the hardest part. There was too much time to think about things. What exact procedures should I follow to reduce my risk of liability? Approach already knew I would accept no one else for runway 25. The Commander pilot was close enough to not want any other plane in a position that could cause a go-around, and I agreed. Just one miscued transmission could create a misunderstanding or lead the pilot astray, and everyone from the FAA administrator to the local anchor on the evening news would be replaying the tape of our conversation from now until Christmas. I rehearsed, giving myself a mental pep talk: When he comes on the frequency, make sure everything is absolutely right the first time; you may not get a second chance. Thoughts of another plane, an F-100, briefly flashed through my mind.

The arrival controller's voice over the intercom brought me back to the moment: "He's eight miles out, straight in to runway seven. Comin' to ya." From now on, every word that any of us said might end up being scrutinized by a dozen different lawyers, so the off-the-wall and occasionally raunchy or forbidden comments made between controllers stopped.

On initial contact, the pilot repeated to me what he had already told arrival control. He had to land on runway 7 and he could not accept any delay or go around. I've since forgotten his exact words, but his tone of voice made it clear that he wasn't kidding. I was ready. There wasn't a moving airplane within several hundred yards of "his" runway. If he ended up going around, it would not be because of anything I would do.

I cleared the Commander to land on runway 7, issued the pertinent wind information, and asked the pilot one more time if he needed any additional assistance or equipment standing by the runway. He replied, "Negative!" As his airplane came into view, we watched and waited. Those of us watching from the tower felt the familiar feeling of helplessness once again.

Less than a quarter of a mile from the runway, and everything we could see looked normal. Each of us must have been thinking, "Just a few hundred more feet and everything should be okay." Seconds later the Commander gracefully touched down on the approach end of runway 7, its flight and presumably its problem over. But with unusual, almost uncomfortable speed, the pilot taxied to the hangar, where first he and then the passengers left the plane and went into the building. For us, the emergency was over. In spite of the emotional seesaw we had been riding for the last fifteen or twenty minutes, it was time to get back to the rest of the traffic.

Before long, a phone call from the pilot solved the mystery of what had happened. Sometime during the previous evening, his taste buds had drawn him inexorably to Loma Linda's, the local Mexican restaurant near the airport. Known by the airline crews who overnighted in Toledo, Loma Linda's had long been accepted as THE place to eat after a long day's flight. One crew even asked for the closest runway to their gate so they could land and get parked before the restaurant closed. As they taxied in, the captain asked me if it was really as good as he had heard. Being rather conservative in my culinary tastes, I answered, "Definitely, if you can stand the smell!" To which he countered rather sarcastically, "Thanks, you just made my day." His airliner, of course, was equipped with two things that the Rockwell Commander didn't have—a copilot and a bathroom.

The Commander pilot revealed that chicken enchiladas spiced with hot, hot sauce had led directly to the priority handling incident. Somewhere over Fort Wayne, Indiana, his lower digestive tract conspired with the rest of his body to organize a violent rebellion. Evidently they collectively decided that twelve or more hours of containing a spicy time bomb was enough. Something had to be done, and the sooner the better.

It became uncomfortably clear to our pilot that one way or another he would have to resort to drastic measures. Either he could land at the nearest airport for a pit stop, which would have done precious little to impress the harried executives sitting in the back, or he could try to hold on until he got home. About thirty miles from Toledo, it because painfully obvious to him that he had made the wrong decision. In the world of corporate flying, where failure to procure the freshest doughnuts can easily lead to a pilot's dismissal, his dilemma could have caused serious results. Five or ten more minutes in the air could have meant the end of an otherwise spotless flying career.

After our official and slightly unorthodox investigation of the incident, the cause was determined to be "pilot error." Extenuating circumstances were considered, just punishment decided, and recommendations to prevent a reoccurrence were offered. The pilot's past history of cooperation and conformity with the air traffic system demanded leniency. The indelible mark the incident left on his memory indicated that the likelihood of a similar situation happening again was remote. All we had to do was decide the proper punishment. For the next couple of weeks, snide comments like "How about some lunch at Loma Linda's before you take off?" were said to have been heard on various frequencies around Toledo.

To his enormous credit, our friend always took the kidding as it was intended, in good fun. Yet I suspect it was a long time before he forgot that carbon monoxide was not the only deadly gas that could incapacitate a pilot in flight. As for me, I learned that helping pilots in the midst of a crisis was one of the things I liked best about my job.

There were other moments, too, that made me realize there are real living, breathing people on both sides of the microphone. New pilots seldom talk to controllers any more than necessary for fear of saying something that will get them into trouble. Corporate pilots tend to be almost as closed-mouthed, most likely because passengers are often close enough to hear what is said from the cockpit. But airline crews can be another matter. While most of the time they are all business, these pilots are confident enough in their professionalism and their ability to have some fun with what goes on.

I remember a particular Thanksgiving Day in Toledo, a slow dreary Thursday made even slower by the reduced holiday schedule. As the Allegheny DC-9 pushed back from the gate preparing to taxi to the runway, the cockpit windows on each side of the jet slowly and unobtrusively opened. Out of the copilot's window came a brightly colored bunch of five or six helium balloons on a string. Out of the captain's window came a plucked, stuffed, and, we assumed, ready-to-bake rubber turkey. As friends and relatives waved good-bye to their loved ones on board, there hung the ornaments, flapping in the breeze all the way out to the runway. On ground control frequency, nothing was said by either party. The actions spoke for themselves. I could only imagine what went through the minds of those left behind. The waving gave way to some rather strange and unsettled looks.

Another memorable moment involved Ron Gettig, a close friend with whom I was working in the tower. Ron was a good old southern boy with an accent to match, and anytime he kidded around on the frequency, his southern drawl made whatever he said sound funnier. Whenever I planned to go flying south of the Mason-Dixon line, I would ask Ron to go along as my spokesman and interpreter.

Since Toledo's airline traffic was rather limited, after a while all the controllers became very familiar with the flight numbers, the types of aircraft used, and the destination of all the planes. Since a typical inbound or outbound rush consisted of two Uniteds, two Easterns, one Allegheny, and a Delta, the task wasn't as difficult as it might seem. This day the United 737 flight that had always left Toledo destined for Chicago's O'Hare Airport was instead heading for Billings, Montana.

That in itself might not have seemed completely foreign to us, but a recent news event must have started Ron's mind working. A few weeks earlier, a United flight from Chicago to somewhere on the West Coast had taken an unusual diversion. It seemed that the flight attendant was one meal short when passing out hot meals to the flight crew, and the captain hadn't gotten any dinner. Apparently fed up with this and, I suspect, a few other frustrations, the captain made an unscheduled stop at a small airport somewhere in the Rockies, went into the airport, and had dinner while the passengers waited on the airplane. When the flight finally reached its original destination, United officials had a few things to say to their well-fed, if not terribly diplomatic, pilot.

When our United flight started to taxi to the runway, Ron casually confirmed that they were headed for Billings instead of Chicago. The copilot replied, "Affirmative, we have an unscheduled stop to make today." To which Ron replied, "What's the matter, captain gettin' kinda hungry already?" From that point until they left our airspace, whenever one of them tried to talk on the radio all we heard was uncontrollable laughter.

It wasn't the first or the last time that Ron used his easygoing manner to get away with things the rest of us just couldn't pull off. There was another particular day when an airliner requested to take off on our short runway. The advantage of using runway 16 was that taxi time from the gate to the runway was about fifteen seconds. The disadvantage was that if the wind, temperature, and humidity weren't especially conducive to flight, the end of the runway could arrive much sooner than an unwary pilot might think. When the crew asked specifically for runway 16, I had no choice but to "issue the wind" (advise the pilot of the current wind direction and speed) and give a go-ahead.

About two-thirds of the way into its takeoff roll, the jet looked as though it was still moving at a snail's pace. Feet off the console, Ron and I stood to watch the takeoff. With just seventy-five to a hundred feet of runway left, the airliner finally became airborne. Before telling the pilot to contact departure, Ron commented that the runway must have looked a little short toward the end. The pilot nonchalantly answered, "Naw, we had a little vibration in the nosewheel and we held it down on the runway to check it out." Ron had his response: "I can tell you what it was. It was probably the copilot's feet trembling on the rudder pedals!" Once again laughter filled the airwaves, and off they went on their way.

We had our share of unexpected situations that kept things interesting, and not all involved air carrier pilots. An unusually high number of situations seemed to happen with Mooney pilots. These are not aviators who belong to some strange religious sect, although they may occasionally see themselves that way, but pilots who fly Mooney airplanes. And there is nothing inherently wrong with airplanes manufactured by the Mooney people. It's just the opposite; the airplanes are almost too well designed and well made. They are fast, sleek-looking machines that are relatively simple to operate and can still be slowed down to a reasonable speed for landing. As much as an airplane can be, a Mooney is all things to all people. Therein lies the problem.

Business men and women and other professional types who know that time and money are valuable and that taking risks is the only way to get ahead often find themselves in the cockpit of a Mooney. In the exacting world of aviation, though, few things are as simple as they seem. Frequently a risk taken can come back to bite the unwary adventurer. Ask almost any air traffic controller which pilots are most likely to end up in a compromising situation and the answer will more than occasionally be Mooney pilots. Fortunately, the airplanes are so well made that pilots usually escape to try their luck again.

Take the Mooney pilot who ran out of fuel near Toledo and landed gear-up in a cornfield not far from the airport. He escaped without injury, and a day or two later we saw his airplane going down the highway on the back of a flatbed trailer. Not long after the plane was repaired, an almost identical situation occurred with very similar results. Not long after that, the airplane was back in the air with its pilot spreading varying degrees of terror wherever he flew. Finally, out of respect for the airplane as much as anything else, the poor, accident-prone pilot's license was suspended, and we all breathed a sigh of relief. Unfortunately, reinforcements were just over the horizon.

It happened one bright, sunny afternoon when only an occasionally disoriented student pilot was temporarily disrupting an otherwise normal flow of traffic. The pilot called approach control about eighteen miles northeast of Toledo, inbound to the airport. Almost as an afterthought, he mentioned that his oil pressure was starting to get low. The controller, evidently more concerned about the potential problem than the pilot, suggested that maybe he should consider using Wagon Wheel Airport, a small but well-maintained airport within gliding distance of his present position. The pilot decided that Toledo was where he had intended to land and that was where he still wanted to go. The controller honored his request and offered radar vectors to the airport.

About three or four miles from the approach end of runway 25, the neglected engine must have decided it had taken enough abuse for one day, and it promptly quit. Very shortly thereafter the pilot appropriately decided it must be time to land. The question was, would it be on the runway or some less suitable location. Since we'd just accepted responsibility for and control of the airplane, those of us in the tower were just as anxious to know the answer.

When we spotted the crippled plane a few miles east of the airport, its chances of reaching the runway seemed doubtful, but we still thought the pilot could pull it off. Soon afterward, in spite of all the mental and verbal urging we could provide, we knew the guy wasn't going to make it. The reason was the concrete bridge about a half-mile east of the airport that served westbound cars on the Ohio Turnpike. It wasn't meant for airplanes. Exactly where the Mooney would land was up for grabs, but it wouldn't be at the airport. As pilot and plane dropped below our line of sight for the last time, we looked at each other with one thought in mind, "Shit!"

As our composure returned, we enlisted the assistance of a flight instructor who happened to be in the airport traffic pattern practicing takeoffs and landings with a student. We asked him to extend his flight path a little farther east so he could see the struggling pilot and let us know how serious the situation was. As we anxiously waited for our answer, the seconds once again seemed to linger interminably. Then we heard the instructor's jubilant response: "He's made it! He's down and safe on the turnpike!" Moments later, out from under the westbound underpass came our Mooney, easin' on down the road with all the rest of the weary travelers.

The scene was as silly as it was pleasing, and for the moment at least our troubles were over. From what we later gathered, this was not the case for the errant pilot. In many states, the authorities frown upon pilots who use superhighways as runways regardless of the reasons. Ohio was no exception. As the entourage of highway patrol cars, turnpike maintenance vehicles, tow truck, and the lone Mooney slowly moved down the turnpike to the first official off-road facility eight miles away, the pilot's bills for his adventure mounted with extraordinary speed. By the time the Mooney found its way back to home base on a flatbed truck, the total bill for inconveniencing the great state of Ohio exceeded a couple of thousand dollars.

TWO ENGINES, TWO STRIKES

THE MOONEY MOTOR HOME WAS A LIGHTER MOMENT IN AIR TRAFFIC CONTROL HISTORY, but there's usually nothing light when an airplane goes down. Almost as certain as death and taxes, if controllers stay controllers long enough, the odds are good that they will eventually get caught in an imminent crisis. How they react and how fate decrees the final outcome can have a lot to do with the rest of their careers.

For more than one good controller, losing a pilot has meant losing that sense of immortal infallibility that helped make the job a little easier. The thought that each decision made could have disastrous consequences moves slightly closer to the conscious surface.

For one friend it happened quickly, almost mercifully and without warning. The pilot of the single-engine plane was on an instrument flight plan, although the weather was good and the operation had been routine all the way. Pat, the controller working the arrival south radar position, had been giving the pilot radar vectors for a visual approach to Toledo.

Radar vectors, or vectors, as controllers commonly refer to them, represent compass directions. They are the most basic means by which controllers direct pilots as they fly. Straight north is 360 degrees. Proceeding clockwise, each degree represents a different course a pilot can fly. If a controller advises a pilot to fly a heading of zero two zero, that vector tells the pilot to proceed in a northeast direction.

For the past hour or so I had been working the handoff position for Pat, assisting him in any way that I could. If that meant asking other controllers for the use of some of their airspace, I would to it. If it meant answering queries from the tower controllers about arriving traffic, I would do that too. Essentially I was to take care of all the extra duties a radar controller normally has so Pat could concentrate his attention on the targets, or airplanes, on his scope.

With light traffic and no reason to expect any problems, I was paying some attention to Pat's traffic in case any assistance was needed. I was also answering occasional questions from a few visitors who were touring the radar room. Suddenly—in the few seconds it took for the radar antenna to rotate 360 degrees, hit the airplane with another burst of energy, and update that plane's location—something happened.

Both the large transponder reply (the on-screen result of a signal transmitted from the airplane) and the smaller primary target (the blip representing the returned energy from the radar antenna) were gone. Although occasionally the transmitter in the airplane or the circuitry in our radar system momentarily caused the display's loss of one signal or the other, the way both of these replies disappeared from Pat's radarscope immediately caught our attention.

No matter how hard we looked or how much we tried to increase the power output of the radar, where moments before an airplane had been, now there was simply nothing. Pat's repeated attempts to reestablish communications with the pilot were equally fruitless.

Nothing was certain. The speed with which the target disappeared seemed to indicate a midair collision, but neither of us could recall another target anywhere in the vicinity. Compounding the problem were our visitors. Normally, at the slightest indication that something was awry, a controlled pandemonium would have enveloped the radar room. Pat would have immediately called for a supervisor to begin directing the ensuing operation.

In the case of a possible midair, like Pat's, the supervisor would usually have a dozen different factors to contend with and as many different duties to fulfill. The radar room's noise level would almost imperceptibly begin to increase with repeated attempts to contact the pilot on the emergency frequency. Without our visitors, I would have instinctively yelled for someone to bring me a grease pencil so I could mark the radarscope with the exact location the airplane was last known to be flying, and Pat would have been talking continually into his boom microphone, almost yelling too, as though a louder voice would be better heard on the missing pilot's radio. As it was, our guests prevented almost all of that from happening.

What, after all, is the appropriate thing to say to folks who have come to observe an example of the world's safest and most efficient air transportation system. "Ah, pardon me ladies and gentlemen, but you will have to excuse us for a few minutes. It seems we have inadvertently lost an airplane somewhere. Nothing to be alarmed about. It's probably just a simple midair collision or some other minor problem." Under the guise that we needed total concentration to deal with an inbound rush, which would never actually materialize, we ushered our guests quickly up to the tower for a different view of the airport.

Then we went back to what had become the decidedly morbid business of trying to find our missing pilot. Three or four more times, Pat tried in vain to contact the pilot. We also notified the highway patrol and the local police that a plane crash might have occurred. So far no one had called either about any airplanes falling uncontrollably from the sky. It had been only a few minutes since the disappearance, but when an airplane accident happens, the public is incredibly quick to respond. On more than one occasion, word of a lost plane has passed from an observer to the authorities to a news reporter and culminated with a phone call to the tower for verification before our people in the front office ever got wind of the situation. The absence of any bad news was the only good news we had to go on.

The next step was as inevitable as it was uncomfortable, maybe because it made the whole situation a little more real. Pat picked the airplane closest to the point of disappearance and asked its pilot if he had heard any distress calls on the frequency. Line-of-sight radio transmissions sometimes allow nearby pilots, but not us, to hear a pilot in trouble, flying at a lower altitude than normal.

Once Pat asked his question, it meant the word was out. Every pilot on the frequency and every eavesdropper with a radio scanner now knew something had gone wrong. They just didn't know exactly what or where, but then neither did we. We did know the tape was running and that everyone within earshot of the ensuing conversation would be straining to find out what happened. If it turned out to be juicy enough, a few of those same people would be contacting the FAA for their own personal copies of the voice recordings, and Pat would be an unwilling star of the drama. The pilot he questioned, however, had heard nothing.

Although discussing an accident on the frequency is the least-liked thing anyone involved with aviation has to do, the time for hedging our bets was over. Lives could easily be saved or lost depending upon how quickly help could be summoned to the scene of the accident. The problem was, we still didn't know where it was or even if there was one. Pat did the only thing he could. He told the pilot that an airplane had disappeared from his radarscope and asked if he would try to help us locate where it went down. As almost every pilot would, he graciously agreed to delay his flight and look for the downed plane.

Predictably, within minutes of Pat's first conversation on the radio, the phones in the radar room began ringing and ringing. At each ring we, and most of all Pat, felt the knot tighten a little more. It seemed only a matter of time before one of the calls would be the answer to all of our questions, and none of us was quite sure we were ready for it. Amid all the commotion, Pat was still sitting at his scope, determinedly vectoring our nameless assistant in the air to the precise spot where the missing airplane had been last seen on radar. When he arrived over the area, there wasn't even the slightest trace that anything unusual had occurred in the field below.

There was nothing else to do but wait. The frantic activities of the past twenty-five minutes were over. In their place came a strained silence, as we gathered our own thoughts and emotions together. Loneliest of all was Pat, sitting quietly, still looking at the radarscope, wondering what had gone wrong and what he should have or could have done differently. A happy, sensitive, thoughtful man who cherished everyone he knew was living a nightmare that would be all but impossible to forget.

Once more the ringing phone brought us to our senses.

Another two or three minutes of suspense and our mystery was over. This call was from the missing pilot. A sudden and total electrical failure had rendered him completely incommunicado. Although there had never been any danger of crashing, the loss of both his radios and his transponder left him totally incapable of informing us of his predicament. According to the government regulations pertaining to just such a situation, he had acted in exactly the proper manner. He landed at the first available airport where he could do so legally, even without a radio. He apologized for the inconveniences he felt he had undoubtedly caused. We reassured him that he had done all the right things and thanked him profusely for calling the radar room. In short, that was that, almost.

With the announcement came a different kind of activity, one borne of relief, spreading throughout the radar room. Barbs began flying back and forth across the room. Al shook his finger at Pat and scoldingly mimicked a parent chastising a child for some dastardly deed: "Son, don't you EVER do that to me again!" Someone else yelled, "See, I told you you couldn't run two together even if you tried." With each jab Pat's smile grew wider and wider. Although the feelings of a few moments earlier would not easily be forgotten, at least for now it was over. And no one, not even the pilot, was more relieved than Pat.

The pilot had known all along that he was in no immediate danger. Without that luxury, Pat had hoped for the best but imagined the worst. In spite of the obvious relief he was now feeling, the past twenty-five minutes had taken their toll. Anyone caught in a situation of feeling responsible for another person's life knows at least some of Pat's emotions. My moment wouldn't come until many months later. Ron wasn't to be as lucky.

Like most controllers, Ron had a nickname. Whether a controller's nickname is based on a physical or personality trait or just on operating initials, over the years each nickname has proved to be unique and uncannily accurate. There was Gomer, whose "Goollly!" was as much Jim Nabors' as his own. There was Chicken Neck, self-explanatory. There was Shithead, seemingly appropriate at first meeting, not really true if anyone took the time to know the real person. And there was one we used repeatedly to describe trainees in various frustrating stages of their controller training. It was simply Stone. Certain trainees occasionally were no smarter than the average rock. Whenever one made an excessively ill-advised control decision, he was rewarded with a large stone attached to a piece of rope. For the remainder of the shift, this fine jewelry hung around his neck as a reminder of his sin. Ron had earned his nickname by how he treated these trainees. He was known, not so affectionately, as the Hawk.

The Hawk was a slight little man with large, heavy, black-rimmed glasses that seemed to cover much more of his face than was necessary for adequate vision. At first glance he could easily have been mistaken for a casting director's idea of the small-town banker, like the one who quivered uncontrollably as Butch and Sundance blew up the safe in front of his eyes. Ron's demeanor, however, was anything but reticent, particularly when it came to trainees. Whenever he worked with a budding controller, Ron always took up the same stance and remained poised that way for the entire session, regardless of how long that session might be. Standing ever so slightly right of the poor soul he was watching, the Hawk would place his right foot on top of the desktop console in front of the radarscope, his left arm on the controller's chair, and hunch over his shoulder, prepared to leap and bark orders whenever he felt the need arise, which would invariably be quite often. In truth, he looked a good bit more like Snoopy perched atop his doghouse and acting "the Vulture" instead of the keen-eyed hawk, but either way the trainee knew a predator was waiting close by, eager to strike.

But when we least expected it, something decided to strike back at Ron, and it hit hard. The end of an evening shift in any radar room is almost always a time to wind down from the activities for which controllers get paid—keeping all the airplanes from hitting one another. This is especially true of the smaller airports around the country, and Toledo was no exception. The air carrier fleet, all six of them, that would overnight in Toledo were safely tucked away for the evening, with most of their crews presumably well through the second course at Loma Linda's. The general aviation pilots too had all called it a day, and even the majority of our corporate pilots, who usually brought their captains of industry home long after everyone else had ceased working, were in the hangars, carefully stowing the last bottles of twelve-year-old Scotch until the next crises arose. The nation's skies now belonged to cargo pilots.

Most of these "fly by night" pilots were young men and women trying to climb the steps of the aviation ladder. Having spent the previous year or two in small, loud, single-engine trainers instructing fledgling pilots in the mysteries of flight, they had moved on. More often than not, the move was into a twin-engine craft only slightly larger and twice as noisy as the previous habitat had been. More often than not, the airplane of choice was a Twin Beech. A classic of sorts, the Twin Beech has been around since the very early days of aviation. Its two large radial engines, quality construction, proven record in a hostile environment, and relatively low price tag made it the ideal airplane for moving substantial amounts of mail and cargo, even if its ambience was somewhat less than elegant.

At about ten o'clock, one of these pilots finished loading his nightly supply of mailbags, climbed into his airplane, and taxied out for takeoff. Although usually alone, the captain of the old Twin Beech had a passenger along for the ride this evening. Friends can help pilots wile away otherwise long quiet nights and maybe get some free flying time to add to their own logbooks. Old or new, twin time was expensive and hard to come by, and flying most of the night seemed a small price to pay for anyone still trying to move up to that next step. As an added bonus, the incredibly clear night sky promised an evening of indescribable serenity and unmatched beauty. As they began what would most likely be their long takeoff roll, all but the most jaded of observers secretly wished for a front row seat in the aging plane.

Although from the radar room we could see nothing, the distinctive throaty roar of the Beech's radial engines at takeoff power signaled the beginning of the next leg of the night run. As with every other departure, rather than gracefully lifting into the air the heavily loaded mail plane grudgingly gave up its hold on gravity and slowly climbed over the trees into the darkness. About a mile from the airport, with little more than the altitude needed to clear the towers and hills below, the pilot checked in with Ron on departure control. After his perfunctory "radar contact, climb and maintain four thousand, proceed on course," Ron and the rest of us went back to talking of everything and nothing.

The pilot's first call came when he was little more than seven or eight miles from the airport. Though the tone of his voice indicated serious concern, none of us sensed that anything more threatening was about to happen. For whatever reason, one of the Twin Beech's two engines had quit. The pilot advised us that he was "feathering" the prop, but he still needed vectors via the most direct route back to the runway at Toledo. With that, Ron and everyone else in the radar room straightened up and immediately reacted to the pilot's request.

Depending upon the specific airplane, the weather conditions, and a host of other variables, the loss of an engine can be anything from a minor inconvenience to certain disaster. Unlike those airplanes we traditionally classify as airliners, which have to be able to lose one, two, or even three engines and still fly well enough to return for landing, smaller twins are not necessarily or even frequently designed with those same characteristics. The truth is, light twins are statistically substantially more dangerous than their single-engine counterparts. For many pilots, one aviation adage says it all: In a twin-engine airplane, when the first engine quits, the second one is just there to get you to the scene of the accident faster. Or as an old aviation friend of mine once put it, "Give me a plane where I can feather one, three, and five, and still keep flying, and I'll show you a good airplane."

The reasons for these feelings and statistics are about as numerous as the variables that cause them. Every airplane ever made is the result of dozens of compromises. Some give up the ability to carry a lot of weight so they can go faster; others give up a great amount of stability in order to be highly maneuverable; and almost all airplanes are designed to carry a full load of fuel, passengers, and/or cargo, but seldom all at the same time. Obviously, when a single-engine airplane loses its engine, it will be landing sometime in the immediate future. It is not so obvious that the same is true for a twin with only one working engine. Exactly when, how, or if the landing will happen is something that even the pilot doesn't always know.

When one of the two engines on the Twin Beech quit, the pilot already had two strikes against him, and both he and Ron knew it. The airplane, though not overloaded, was literally as full of cargo as the law would allow. Its long takeoff roll and subsequent slow, gradual climb to four thousand feet indicated that every bit of horsepower available was being used to sustain the climb. When half of that power was suddenly taken away, it was clear that a continued climb would be impossible. The only question was, would the remaining engine be able to keep plane and passengers in level flight? For many light twins, loaded to capacity, the answer is usually no. The descent to the earth below may be slowed somewhat by a good engine, but before long a crippled twin has to land.

Ron did exactly what any of us would have done. He issued the pilot a heading that would take him directly to the approach end of runway 25, and—not knowing how the dead engine would affect the turning characteristics of the Beech—Ron told the pilot to turn either left or right to get to that heading. Almost immediately we became painfully aware of what might become the third strike. In a voice suddenly filled with a straining sense of urgency, the pilot advised Ron that he couldn't feather the propeller on the useless engine. The long, fat blades that until a few minutes ago had been slicing up huge chunks of air and turning them into thrust, now could not be stopped.

Had the pilot been able to feather the propeller on the failed engine, it would have created less resistance to the oncoming wind. With feathering, each blade would have been mechanically turned sideways so only the thin edge faced directly into the wind. In addition, the rotation of the entire propeller would have been stopped by locking it into one position, lessening the wind resistance even more. With one quick action, the pilot would have been able to increase significantly the distance his faltering plane might have glided.

Instead, those big fat propeller blades became almost a solid large shield as they slowly windmilled through the air. The increased drag and the resulting loss of aerodynamic efficiency meant only one thing. The Twin Beech was coming down, very soon.

Had the pilot been at a higher altitude, the unfeathered prop may not have been cause for serious concern. The weather was good and the pilot most likely had never lost sight of the runway since the beginning of his flight. He could have used his altitude to maneuver safely to the airport and then glided in, circling down over the runway. But—strike two—he had not even reached his already low cruising altitude of four thousand feet when things started to go wrong. What followed might have been written as the climactic monologue to a Class B adventure movie. The only problem was, it wasn't pretend.

Pilots, like the rest of humanity, react to life-threatening crises in many different ways. Some have neither the desire nor the time to say anything, so they spend their last few moments before impact in silence. Some plead helplessly for any kind of human or supernatural intervention. Still others, like the copilot on the Boeing 727 caught in a midair collision, dutifully maintain their heroic image even in the face of insurmountable odds; his last words on the frequency were "I love ya, Mom." Our Twin Beech pilot began an almost uninterrupted description of what was happening onboard the airplane.

The sense of urgency and ultimate resignation that played on the frequency for the next few minutes will probably remain with those of us who heard them for a good part of our lives. The pilot, obviously struggling to keep his ailing plane in the air, made it terribly clear to us that he couldn't maintain his altitude. To keep the plane at a speed needed for continued flight, he had begun a descent. He told us that he was still trying to feather the one propeller, and then he asked Ron exactly how far away he was from the runway. In spite of his own rising tension, Ron gave the pilot the information he needed. He also told him that the tower controller had been instructed to turn all the runway and approach lights up as high as they would go.

The pilot then started hinting that he didn't think he could make it to the runway. Was there another airport closer? If not, did we know of any other suitable landing site within range? And each time the pilot unkeyed his microphone Ron was there, offering strong words of encouragement in spite of an ever-growing sense of helplessness. Ron's fear was different from that which filled the cockpit several miles away, but it was nonetheless very real. When pilots make mistakes, they are often not around to worry about them, but when controllers make mistakes, they aren't the ones that suffer the loss of life. Ron's life wasn't in any danger, but the sheer desperation of bearing witness to that situation and being unable to affect the outcome can be devastating to even the strongest person. This time no one had really made a mistake, and every time he had a chance to talk, Ron was the reassuring voice that everything would be okay.

But by this time, there wasn't anyone left who truly believed what Ron was so carefully saying. Finally, the pilot began telling us what we didn't want to know. In vivid detail, he described the next

few minutes in the cockpit. They could no longer stay aloft, so he was going to have to land in the darkness below. He was coming down and all he could see ahead were trees, tall trees. The last words we heard were "We're going into the trees, we're not going to make it!" Then, after the briefest sound of impact, there was silence.

Moments later the controller in the tower called down on the intercom and said he had just seen a bright flash where the Twin Beech had been. As the airplane tore apart, the fuel had ignited and engulfed it in a matter of seconds. The impact itself may have been survivable; the fire that followed wasn't. Pilot and passenger both died in the crash. We sat there in uncomfortable silence. Fire and police teams were already being sent to the scene and each of us hoped for the best, but I think we already knew what they later confirmed.

For us, at least for the moment, it was over. All that was left were the lingering memories, the terrible thoughts about what we might have done to change the ending and the even more painful process of imagining what those few moments in the cockpit were like. Whether in the controllers' breakroom, or in the church pews, or just in our minds, that terrible evening would be replayed countless times over. In one way or another, each of us would never be the same again.

HOW YOU SAY IT

IF ONE ASPECT OF THE JOB IS THE VERY HEART OF BEING A CONTROLLER, it's communication. Controllers receive information from dozens of different sources. They interpret, assimilate, relay, and otherwise disseminate that same information in as many different ways as it was first received.

If they do it accurately, concisely, and efficiently, pilots, other controllers, and supervisors all remain relatively safe and happy. If they fail to communicate at critical moments, a good day can turn exceedingly sour exceedingly fast. Hence, one of the first and most important maxims of air traffic control: What you say is not nearly as important as how you say it. Or put another way, the amount of authority and confidence in a controller's voice is usually inversely proportional to the controller's actual experience and ability to deal with any given situation.

The radio transmissions heard in the lifetime of a single air traffic controller can approach an almost infinite variety of situations, conversations, and dialects. Knowing in advance how to deal with every conceivable incident that might arise is nothing short of impossible. Conveying to pilots the impression that the impossible has indeed been attained, however, can often keep a controller on the winning side of a verbal confrontation.

I have spent my fair share of time parrying attacks as well as

taking the offensive, and I've learned that winning is a lot more fun than losing. One of my more humiliating experiences occurred in 1985 during an evening shift in the tower at Greater Pittsburgh Airport while I was working "Local Two," the position charged with arrivals and departures on runway 28R (right). Because of temporary restrictions initiated shortly after the Professional Air Traffic Controllers Organization (PATCO) strike of 1981, the nature of local controllers' jobs throughout the country had changed significantly. While previously the local controller was concerned only with sending departures on their way one right after another, regardless of destination and with only the appropriate three or five miles of radar separation provided, now a new and improved gimmick had been added.

The imposed restrictions brought with them a new system of bookkeeping that relegated the majority of a controller's time to clerical duties instead of "real" controller chores. Instead of being able to concentrate on weaving a masterpiece of arriving and departing airplanes on and off the runways as fast as was humanly and legally possible, the local controller became a timekeeper and a secretary. Each departing flight had a specified time at which it could take off, and every one of those times had to be duly recorded on at least two separate documents.

Four years later I was still caught in the midst of sorting out airplanes to comply with those "temporary" procedures. Examples: USAir 187 has to pull into the run-up pad and wait for a release time of 2305 Zulu (aviation's term for Greenwich mean time); United 285 can't go until ten minutes after USAir 3, since they're both going out the same airway and the center has restrictions due to bad weather in Chicago; there's flow control into the New York area so Washington will call us back with a release time for People 195—tell him to expect at least a thirty-five-minute delay; finally, tell USAir 236 to be off in exactly three minutes or it's another twenty-minute wait. So it went, as the evening flow of airplanes ready for departure taxied up the hill to runway 28R. (If two runways form parallel lines, one is tagged left and the other right; Pittsburgh had 28L and 28R.)

In the middle of moving airplanes in and out of the run-up pad, around, ahead of, behind, and past one another, I instructed two USAirs to pull into the pad and allow a Company 727 to pass them up. As I did, the captain in one of the delayed airplanes responded, "What's the matter, you like him more than us?" Innocuously I answered, "Naw, that's not it. I like all of you." An innocent remark, but as soon as I said it I knew it had been the wrong thing to do.

There is almost nothing more volatile than a crowd of pilots sitting around in airplanes, all dressed up with no place to go. The routine of preflight preparation long since out of the way, all they have left to do is sit in the limited confines of the cockpit, stare out their small windows, and critically review other pilots' performance while simultaneously listening to the frequency for just the right opportunity to exercise their collective rapier wit. Unfortunately I gave them an opening.

For the next four or five minutes, the remaining crews who were stuck on the ground awaiting departure had a field day with how well I liked them all: "Better be careful, he might ask you out to dinner next time," and "I always thought that one sounded a little too friendly."

A couple of times my thumb started to twitch as it went for the transmit button on my headset control. But then good judgment and the lack of anything clever enough to say to quell the disturbance stopped me. I stood there feeling my face get redder and redder with each stinging comment, but I knew that to say more would only make matters worse. I had been had and all I could do was stand there and take it. My only consolation was that sooner or later someone else somewhere would make a bigger fool of himself than I just had.

Before too many days passed, my prayers began to be answered. Larry, a new controller in training on ground control, was the first to take the heat off me. In a single two-hour training session, this poor lad wiped the slate clean for at least a couple of us who had previously paved the way before him. If there is one control position in a terminal radar approach facility that breeds contempt and loathing in the hearts of air traffic controllers everywhere, it's ground control. At a busy airport it can best be compared to playground duty at a school for hyperactive children. Everyone wants to do something and they all want to do it right now!

Pilots also tend to view ground controllers with an emotion that is about two or three steps below disdain. An independent lot to begin with, professional pilots have come to accept "federal assistance" in the air as a necessity for doing business in the increasingly crowded skies. They don't always like it, but they almost all agree that air traffic controllers are necessary. However, the same cannot be said for their accepting direction on the ground.

There are times when it seems a bit presumptuous to advise a pilot to follow the Boeing 747 just ahead when the laws of physics make it highly inappropriate to do anything else. On the other hand, I have witnessed countless occasions when, in the heat of a heavy departure rush, two or more pilots tried to occupy the same space at the same time in spite of the ground controller's admonitions. No matter which pane of glass you're looking through, sometimes the ground at an airport can be one of the unfriendliest places in the world.

Ground problems are further complicated by too little maneuvering room at many airports around the country. Pittsburgh airport, originally commissioned around 1952, was typical. It had too little concrete and too many airplanes. As the terminal building grew to accommodate increasing numbers of passengers and planes, the ramp and taxiway space outside the building became smaller and smaller. Just two or three poorly positioned airplanes could easily shut down the entire operation indefinitely.

Larry's situation turned ugly all too fast. Thirty or so airplanes had pushed back from their gates at just about the same time. All but two or three of them belonged to USAir, and most of those twenty-seven or twenty-eight looked alarmingly similar. If Larry didn't remember which DC-9 was which as it pushed back from the gate, the odds were good that things would only go downhill from there. Unfortunately, his memory wasn't all that good at the moment.

As the departures started maneuvering toward the runway, Larry realized he desperately needed to move the third DC-9 in a string of about ten. The problem was that, try as he might, he just couldn't remember its callsign.

Larry should have said something like "DC-9 directly abeam gate thirty-six at the south tip, say your number." At which point the pilot most likely would have answered and the problem would have been at least partially resolved. But in the heat of battle, logic doesn't always come charging to the forefront. Instead, Larry chose what no doubt seemed to him a coherent course of action. He said,

"I want the DC-9 who is behind the DC-9 in front of you to flash your lights." He hoped thus to identify the flight number and move some airplanes.

There was just one minor setback. No one sitting out on the ramp and none of us in the tower had the slightest idea what he was talking about. Almost immediately there were more flashing DC-9 lights than we could count. Undaunted, Larry moved on to phase two of his plan. (At one time or another every controller working ground who was up to his eyeballs in airplanes has wanted to say it. Until Larry, none dared do it.) After carefully assessing the situation, he calmly keyed his microphone and said, "Everybody who is ready, taxi to runway 28R."

Although the entire ramp was clogged with airplanes, up until now the whole thing had been mildly amusing. That one transmission, however, changed the character and the likely outcome. Telling a group of tired, frustrated, and already late pilots to taxi en masse to one runway was about as efficient and safety oriented as running ahead of the bulls in the streets of Pamplona during the Fiesta of San Fermin. It might work out in the end, but it probably wouldn't be a pretty sight.

As the whine of about seventy jet engines simultaneously spooling up filtered through the glass panes in the tower, Ken Erb, supervisor on duty, made a mad dash for his headset, which was sitting on the ledge in the back of the tower cab. Within seconds he was plugged into the second ground control position, yelling to the crowd milling about outside, "Everyone on the ramp, stop where you are NOW!" After thirty-five minutes of hair-pulling confusion, some semblance of order returned to the airport. About half of the departing airplanes were already on their way, and the rest were lined up in a neat row on the taxiway awaiting their turns for the runway ahead. As for Larry, he learned that there is one trick he should never pull out of the bag again.

Larry's trick was really more of an honest mistake or an error in judgment, common for someone of his experience level. Every once in a long while an experienced pilot or controller takes the game a little too far. There was, in Toledo, an old barnstormer known throughout the region as one of the pioneers of aviation in the Midwest, who simply hated the FAA and anyone associated with it. Every new controller had to learn that whenever this man came on the frequency, he was out to make the worst of any situation. He was an excellent pilot, though, and was almost always able to pull it off without actually hurting anyone.

He had his own little list of tricks: never answering a call on the frequency unless absolutely necessary, never identifying himself or his airplane number when initiating a call to a controller, and never giving a controller any warning when he was planning to do something until it was done. Yet he was extremely well versed in the regulations, which he despised, and never stepped over the line far enough to require legal intervention. He was, in truth, more of an irritation than a hazard, until one day when many of us felt he went a little too far.

It was a bitterly cold day, tempered only by the bright sunshine and the brilliant blue winter sky. Although the runway had been plowed and sanded, it was still mostly snow-covered, with only an occasional patch of concrete showing through here and there. Pilots reported the braking action as fair to good, and in spite of their ongoing efforts, the snow removal crews could do little else to improve conditions until the temperature rose. Alongside of and in between the runways and the taxiways, the snow was piled three to four feet high. Winter had settled for a long stay in Ohio.

With no advance notice from approach control—this pilot never took advantage of the radar service available—the tower controller working local control received his first call from the inbound pilot: "I'm five miles east inbound for landing."

The voice was all too familiar, but the controller didn't know which of the airplanes based at his hangar our senior aviator was flying, so he had to ask for the identification number. The pilot answered and local gave him clearance to land on runway 25. The pilot responded with, "Can't land on two five."

As the game began, the local controller asked the obvious question: "I understand you can't land on runway two five. What's the problem?"

The answer, "No wheels. I need to land in the snow."

"Are you declaring an emergency?"

"No, I'm not. I just need to land in the snow beside the runway."

What should have been a simple operation on a slower-than-average day suddenly because a complex legal entanglement. At every public airport in the country, only certain areas are designated as approved landing sites, most commonly referred to as runways. In spite of this fact, pilots try, and occasionally succeed at, landing on every other piece of paved and nonpaved, flat and not-so-flat parcel of ground around those airports. This upsets the FAA, the county government, and every other legal authority even remotely associated with the airport's operation.

In emergency conditions, controllers do have the authority to approve a landing at whatever location the pilot deems necessary, as long as the pilot is aware that he or she is assuming the liability for risk. Our present situation, however, didn't seem to fit that bill. The local controller told our veteran aviator to circle east of the airport until approval for his request could be obtained from the county. In an unusually delighted tone, he replied, "Roger!"

After a few minutes of consultation, the airport manager decided that if the pilot said he had to land in the snow he could do it, but not until the emergency equipment was called out and moved to the area on which the pilot would land. Knowing who was in the airplane, the county wasn't about to leave any avenue open through which the pilot could later claim negligence. We relayed the decision to the pilot and advised him to continue circling until the emergency crews were ready.

At the appointed time, local control gave the pilot clearance to proceed inbound and approval to land at his own risk on the snow. Having not yet seen the airplane that was to conduct this unusual maneuver, we all eagerly looked out the tower window for the first sign of our daredevil ace. As soon as his airplane came into sight, we realized the reason for the pilot's insistence that he land on the snow instead of the runway. The plane was on skis.

Plane and pilot had no doubt departed from a surface similar to, if not worse than, that upon which they were about to land. For the skilled pilot, landing an airplane with skis on snow is probably less hazardous than landing an airplane with wheels on a dry runway. The mystery, or rather, the hoax, was over. Had the pilot contacted the airport manager earlier and told him of his plan, the landing could have been handled as a matter of routine. The county would have passed the word to the tower, and we would have given the pilot landing approval with little or no delay.

Instead, a lot of people had been taken away from other important jobs, expensive rescue equipment had been unnecessarily moved out to the landing site, and a potentially disastrous condition had been created, since others truly needing help would have been unable to get it as quickly. Time was wasted, confusion was created, and those of us on the ground were made to look like fools. As the pilot taxied his airplane through the snow to his hangar, he chuckled and said, "Thanks a lot for the assistance, fellas. See you later!"

Other pilots, even (and more often) highly experienced ones, won't ask for the help they really need until it's almost too late. Usually hidden somewhere among their reasons is pride. I suspect pride, combined with a lack of good judgment, had a lot to do with the events of one such evening. We were in the final stages of wrapping up another three-to-eleven shift in the radar room at Toledo. In preparation for the two-person midnight crew that kept Toledo Tower and Toledo Approach Control operating on its twenty-four-hour daily watch schedule, the two radar positions known during busier hours as north and south approach had been combined into one position.

I alone was responsible for all the traffic operating within the airspace just south of Detroit. It extended forty miles either side of Toledo Express Airport on an east-west line, thirty miles south, and about eighteen miles north of the field up to an altitude of eight thousand feet. Although large by the geographical standards allotted to most terminal facilities, Toledo's unusual location seldom caused the size of our airspace to burden its controllers with more airplanes than they could safely handle. Working all the traffic by myself only meant I wouldn't be bothered with trying to share the load with another controller. No matter how relentless the sporadic flow of late-night traffic became, three or four airplanes couldn't keep two radar controllers busy.

I accepted the handoff from the center controller just as the twin-engine Cessna was arriving at our southern boundary. The pilot and passengers enroute to Detroit Metro would fly almost directly northeast to their destination and be out of my area in about fifteen or twenty minutes. The weather was good, and traffic had just about died down for the evening. Under normal circumstances I would only have to interrupt my idle sideline conversations with other controllers once or twice to talk to the pilot.

The questions started with our initial conversation on the frequency. "Approach, how far do you show us from Detroit?" For the next ten or twelve minutes, at regular intervals, several different variations on the same theme became the crux of our discourse. Each time the pilot keyed his mike, the nature of his request became irritatingly more precise. "What runway is Detroit using tonight? Are they running any delays there? How far from the runway are pilots being vectored to the final? Can I get direct to the airport?" With each request, I became less eager to furnish the information. Fortunately, some sense of loyalty made me provide answers to his unending questions. I complied partly because his voice indicated neither arrogance nor belligerence but instead a sincere need to know.

Later, as I looked back to examine the incident, everything that had transpired on the frequency came into focus. What misled me at the time was the complete lack of emotion in the pilot's voice. I sensed little more than a harried pilot forced by passengers, policy, or time into an untenable situation. In that world where time is measured in minutes or fractions of minutes and connections depend upon the exact calculation of both, pilots and controllers are frequently forced into making an apparently impossible situation work. To me, this was just another one of those times. While it might have been the first that day for the pilot, I had heard the same story so many times before it was just the same old words with a slightly different tune.

As the Cessna approached the northern boundary that defined the end of our airspace and the beginning of Detroit Approach Control, I was only too ready to be rid of my constant radio companion. I contacted my counterpart in the TRACON at Metro Airport and transferred control of the plane and pilot to him. Everything was out of my hands for the remainder of the flight. I had only one more thing to do: "Twin Cessna two three hotel, contact Detroit Approach on one one eight point niner five. Good night, sir."

"Roger, Detroit on one one eight point niner five. Thank you, good night."

The end however, turned out to be the beginning. About twelve miles northeast of Toledo on a direct line with Detroit Metro Airport, the pilot, who should have been talking to another approach controller some thirty miles away, called me back five or ten seconds after I had said good-bye, good luck, and leave me alone. "Toledo, this is two three hotel. I'm out of fuel!"

Although some pilot somewhere is always willing to try it,

running out of fuel is seldom a great idea, and doing it at night makes the prospects for a successful outcome even more dubious. Nevertheless, there he was, and to my complete dissatisfaction, there I was. The pilot and his passengers had a lot more to lose than I, but in a very real sense we were in this mess together, like it or not.

Certain emergencies provide a pilot with the greatest of all luxuries, time. Others do not. This one obviously had to be classified as the latter. Without sufficient time, the choice of practical alternatives became equally restrictive. For a couple of gut-wrenching moments, the pilot and I rapidly reviewed the options at hand. The only solution available was Wagon Wheel Airport, about five miles away. I would provide the vectors to line him up with the closest end of the runway. He would provide the expertise to ensure that he arrived at that point with enough altitude to make it.

All that was left was to do it. To that end, I gathered my wits and remembered that old maxim, It isn't so much what you say as how you say it. My hands were shaking and my heart was pounding, but I was not going to let him hear me sweat. I would sound as though I knew exactly how the flight would end, even if I hadn't the slightest idea whether or not we could pull it off.

There were so many things to do so quickly, but none of them would be necessary if either he or I lost control. The first and most important job was to tell the pilot exactly how far from the runway he was. Darkness can easily distort one's perception of distance, and the good visibility that is normally a pilot's strongest ally only makes that distortion greater. Objects that appear to be just ahead are often, in reality, a long distance away. For the pilot faced with an imminent forced landing, nothing would be worse than having enough altitude to reach the safety of a runway but squandering it away prematurely.

The first anyone in the radar room knew of the problem facing us was when they heard my outburst, "The stupid son of a bitch is out of fuel!" The epithet was more of a tension-relieving reaction than an accurate assessment of the pilot's abilities. I was distinctly upset at having to face a dangerous situation in which one bad decision on my part could have potentially fatal results for a group of people I neither knew nor cared about beyond my usual professional concerns. I think I also wanted to proclaim as loudly as possible that what was about to happen was all HIS fault.

My shout also created some extremely helpful by-products. Everyone left in the radar room immediately sprang to life. One controller grabbed his headset, plugged it into the console at the adjacent scope, and began taking the rest of my traffic on another frequency. That left me free to concentrate on the vectors that had to be nearly perfect the first time. Another told Detroit Approach that the airplane they had just accepted would not be coming, and why. A third brought our book of airports to my side and began providing me with information the pilot might need. One more stood by just in case I instantly needed something that no one else had thought to provide.

With as much confidence and reassurance as I could force into my shaky vocal cords, I started working out our plan with the pilot. "Turn right heading one one zero. The airport will be twelve o'clock and five miles. Advise when you have the beacon in sight." His reply, "Roger, I have the beacon. What about the runway lights?"

At most small airports that are unattended during much of the night, the runway lights can be remotely activated. By tuning the radio to a preselected frequency and keying the microphone three to five times, the pilot can turn on the lights and adjust them to various intensities from within the cockpit. Such was the case with Wagon Wheel Airport. The only problem was, I couldn't remember what frequency would do the trick. I yelled out to anyone and everyone in the room who might have the answer. But before I even finished the question, the answer came back. "It's Unicom, one two two point eight!" I relayed it to the pilot, and just as quickly he responded that he had the runway in sight.

I'm not really sure who was reassuring whom, but when I told him he was looking very good for a straight-in approach to the runway he calmly came back with, "Roger, it looks good from here too." But as he arrived on a one-mile final, it became evident that he still had too much altitude to lose for a straight-in approach. He had wisely retained all the altitude possible until certain that he could glide down to the runway. He advised me that he would overfly the airport, enter a close downwind leg, and make a normal, if uncomfortably quiet, pattern to the runway. I continued to keep radio contact with him just to ensure that he knew someone was there and to reaffirm that, from where I sat, his decision looked like a good one.

As the pilot continued his descent lower and lower, he finally reached the point when landing was only moments away. Then he excitedly asked me how long the runway was. Why he hadn't thought to ask for such basic and critical information earlier, I had no idea. Why I didn't think to offer that same information in time for it to be received and digested, I had even less of an inkling.

Though it sounded like the old cliché it was, time was truly running out. Again, one of my faithful partners gave me the information I needed. But this time when I passed it on to the pilot, my voice cracked and showed a hint of the emotion I had so far kept tightly bottled up inside of me. When he answered me, I felt even worse. His voice cracked too. As long as both of us kept telling each other everything was going to be all right, we believed it would be. But as soon as one let out the suggestion that a serious doubt existed, the other was only too ready to carry it to fruition.

At about two or three hundred feet above the ground, his target dropped off the radarscope. All indications were that the twin Cessna was in a good position from which to make it to the runway. After that last brief but emotional conversation, neither of us had said anything more. It was time to sit and wait for the phone call that I hoped would come from the pilot.

Seconds turned into minutes, the minutes began adding up, and still the phone in the radar room didn't ring. I sat staring at the radarscope, saying nothing and waiting. After about ten minutes, we asked the police to drive to the airport and find out what happened. Again, the minutes dragged painfully on as we waited for word. Finally the phone rang, and my pounding heart reverberated through every muscle and bone within me.

Within seconds, before he even finished taking the call, Don gave me a thumbs-up sign from across the room. Although not a soul was anywhere to be found, the airplane was intact and parked on the ramp. The pilot had beaten the odds and made it safely to the runway. Perhaps his not calling had something to do with his violation of more than one federal air regulation. Or maybe he was just too occupied with other matters. I never found out. I'm sure he eventually heard from the FAA, but that night we never received the phone call that could have shortened an agonizing and painful wait.

Admittedly, my part in the unusual landing had been relatively small, but the missing pat on the back from the pilot left me feeling little cause to celebrate what, at least for the moment, seemed a rather unvictorious conclusion to a dramatic beginning. I was angry and bitter, angry that the pilot needlessly prolonged the wait I was forced to endure and bitter that no one seemed to realize how terribly difficult the last fifteen or twenty minutes had been for me.

As always, in retrospect I knew I had learned a couple of valuable lessons that night. Some pilots caught in the midst of a life-threatening series of events rely heavily on the moral support that air traffic controllers can and frequently do offer. A few might even consider that support to be infinitely more valuable than any technical expertise a controller might possess. The other thing I learned was that, while a calm, composed voice may not be the most important assistance controllers provide for pilots in distress, the lack of it can easily undermine the help they might otherwise be able to offer.

23 BRAVO

IF TIME DOESN'T ALWAYS PUT EVENTS IN THEIR PROPER PERSPECTIVE, it at least leaves them in a noticeably more pleasant one. In recalling my most vivid memories as an air traffic controller, I realize it wasn't frequently or even occasionally a thankless job. It was, instead, a great opportunity to work with and for a special combination of very special people.

Of course, I met more than a few bureaucratic boneheads throughout my career, but as often as not I was mercifully insulated from them by at least one or two levels of dysfunctional management designs. All things considered, the saying we used to have—If it weren't for the pilots, this would be a great job—just wasn't true. It was only the pilots and the other controllers that made the job worthwhile. For those many acquaintances I developed throughout the years, I am exceedingly grateful.

But because the existence of a controller is at best a strange one, the relationships came in like fashion. Day after day, controllers talk to hundreds of people without ever seeing or knowing most of them. They affect plans and make decisions, often critical ones, collectively and individually without ever really knowing the other people involved. Most of these conversations are a series of short, occasionally terse transmissions during which every word and every intonation are carefully recorded on the same kind of device that sent Richard Nixon into early retirement. Proper phraseology, using the correct words and abbreviations designated for aviation use, is the key to safety and efficiency. But pilots and controllers are a sometimes clever and independent bunch.

With the passage of time, they develop a sixth sense that enables them to effectively read between the lines of those endless, sometimes boring, transmissions. Words or phrases, apparently randomly dropped, aren't so random after all. In a hundred different ways, they all say the same thing to those involved: Let's get the job done the best way we know how and worry about the regulations later.

By government standards, many of the conversations were "highly irregular," which was really a euphemism for "You're goin' to jail if you keep that up!" And at certain times of the year, the air traffic control frequencies were filled with chatter. Superbowl Sunday was usually one of those times. Minutes after the kickoff, which seemed to come days after the pregame show, radar rooms around the country became clearinghouses for the latest scores, statistics, and instant replay highlights of the latest touchdown drive. The same, of course, was true during the World Series, the Kentucky Derby, the Indy 500, and just about every other major sports event the world had to offer. We felt we had a duty to share information with our community, and occasionally the magnitude of the task was nothing short of awesome.

There were times, and one in particular, when the job of relaying important information wasn't quite as enjoyable. The day the Challenger disaster occurred, those of us working the radar positions felt an obligation to inform the rest of the aviation community that all was not well in the skies over Florida. The news wasn't given out because of some perverse need to capitalize on other people's tragedies, but more because an elite group of aviation pioneers had just perished. However distant the connection between ordinary flying and that accomplished on the fringes of our universe, and however different an airplane pilot might be from a shuttle astronaut, there was still that very real sense of fraternity.

No matter how short the flight or how simple the machine, anyone who has ever flown an airplane alone felt the loss a little more than the rest of the world. Many of us also anticipated what much of the initial public reaction would be, and we knew it didn't bode well for future flights. After my announcement, the frequency turned eerily quiet. The only comment was one pilot's soft "Oh no!"

An irregular conversation for an air traffic control frequency? I guess so, but there were countless others that helped make going to work each day a little easier. There was one airplane, called a "Short's," that seemed to elicit more than its share of unruly comments from other pilots. More often referred to as a Short because no one knows which name is actually correct, it is an odd, awkward-looking flying machine that has found a niche for itself as a short-range commuter airplane. It serves its purpose well, receives high ratings from both pilots and passengers who use it, and no doubt has made a fairly decent profit for its makers. The reason for its propensity to draw unto itself frequent and uninvited abuse is that it is one of the ugliest inventions ever to take to the air.

The Short looks a lot like a pregnant tuna fish, with wheels welded in the down position and a sad, droopy nose that seldom looks like it's having a good day. The fuselage starts out rather sleek and aerodynamic, develops a goiterlike enlargement at its midpoint, and then tapers to a flat, ungainly tail. By any measure, a Short looks as though it should be much more comfortable waddling through a puddle than soaring through the air.

An Eastern Airline captain I was working with one day seemed to share my view. He was number two behind a Short for a visual approach to runway 28L at Pittsburgh. Being number two is a phrase most professional pilots would just as soon strike from their vocabularies. It means wasting valuable fuel and time following number one. Being number two behind a commuter airplane makes the whole ordeal even more distasteful, and when the commuter flight is a Short, insult is added to injury. The captain let me know beyond any doubt that he was insulted.

I vectored the Eastern DC-9 into a position behind the Short, which should have been five miles ahead of the DC-9 at its twelve o'clock position. I told the captain about the traffic he was to follow and asked that he start looking in earnest for the Short. As is often the case around a hub airport that becomes a rendezvous for seventy or eighty airplanes at a time, the Eastern pilot saw one plane here, a couple there, and a few more over on the final, but he couldn't find the Short. With the distance between the two airplanes rapidly diminishing, I could wait no longer for him to see and follow the Short. I issued the captain a turn that would take him away from the plane ahead but would also take him farther away from the airport.

This action, vectoring a pilot away from the airport, often directly correlates with how well the pilot can see traffic ahead. To what phenomenon this miraculous improvement in eyesight can be attributed no one has ever determined, but the easiest way to help a pilot spot heretofore unseen airplanes is to turn him or her away from the area in which they are located. No sooner had the instruction left my mouth than the Eastern captain grumpily replied, "Ah, Approach, we have the Short in sight now. We'll take a visual approach." Only too happy to oblige, I cleared Eastern for a visual approach to follow the Short. The problem was resolved except for a parting shot from the Eastern pilot: "Roger, cleared for the visual and we'll follow the Dempsy Dumpster ahead of us." The ugly duckling had been called a lot of different names before, but the reference to garbage did precious little to please the cockpit crew inside the wounded Short.

Only one other time did I hear a more vicious attack on the frequency, and had I been able to stop laughing long enough to reprimand the perpetrator, I surely would have done so. The end result was funny, but the circumstances that allowed it to occur were not. Not long after a McDonnell-Douglas DC-10 crashed in Chicago because one of its engines fell off, the FAA decided to ground the remaining fleet of DC-10s until it could determine if the cause of the accident was isolated or more widespread. The move temporarily appeased an outraged flying public, but it left Minneapolis-based Northwest Airlines with millions of dollars' worth of big shiny airplanes sitting idly on the ramp at Wold Chamberlain Airport. For an unknown period of time, Northwest's size and influence in the Twin Cities would be reduced to that of its closest competitor, North Central Airlines. North Central would eventually merge with Southern to become Republic Airlines, which would later suffer the ultimate indignity and merge with who else but Northwest Airlines and take that grand old name in aviation as their own.

But before all that happened, a North Central DC-9 captain decided to take a rare opportunity to rub a little salt into the wounds of his larger, more powerful neighbor. Had I not momentarily misplaced the North Central jet as it taxied to runway 29L, an incident probably would not have occurred. Although it might seem difficult, losing something as large as a DC-9 was in keeping with my limited experience as a ground controller at Minneapolis Airport. There were just too many jets that looked too much alike that made one too many trips to the same runway at the same time. The result was the inevitable consequence of what seemed to be the airline's deliberate attempt to confuse me.

When I asked the captain to pinpoint his exact location so I could restore order to my sequence of taxiing airplanes, I can only imagine what must have taken place inside the cockpit during the silence that followed. As the smile slowly crept across his face, he must have thought he had successfully confounded ATC one more time. Then when he looked out the cockpit window to see exactly where he was, that wry smile must have turned into a horrific grin. There, just to his left, sitting row upon row with their bright red tails majestically pointed skyward, was Northwest's fleet of dust-collecting, revenue-eating DC-10s. The North Central pilot must have realized that fate had finally dealt him a winning hand.

"Ah, Ground, we're out here on the parallel to two nine left, just abeam the ah . . . junkyard!"

That was only the beginning. While I silently sat out the next few minutes, pilots from the opposing sides finished off the battle. Volley after volley flew through the air until finally, with their wit and frustration spent, life returned to normal.

Of the countless conversations I had with almost as many unknown pilots, one was of unique importance to me for a variety of reasons. This time I knew who was on the other end of the microphone. He was a wealthy, prominent, and powerful businessman in the Toledo and, I suspect, the national community. As an heir to at least some portion of the Champion Spark Plug Corporation fortune, his lot in life was probably cast at a very early age.

Exactly what his position within the corporate structure was I never knew. If he wasn't the CEO, he probably was close to it. His personal airplane was a Beechcraft King Air, and later, when Cessna introduced the single-pilot version of their popular business jet, he traded in the King Air for a new Citation. Both airplanes were painted with the same distinctive colors as the rest of Champion's fleet of corporate aircraft, and each was as immaculately kept as the glistening hangar floor upon which they sat. To those of us on the outside, the guy gave every appearance of having it made.

Now, without a whole lot of trouble, everyday, ordinary pilots end up measuring a little on the arrogant side of the humility meter. After all, on an almost daily basis many of them defy death with remarkable consistency, and they do it as a matter of course. Add to that already overconfident profile a position in the business world requiring frequent high-level, large-scale decision making, and all the necessary ingredients are there for that person to be a royal pain in the neck.

Every controller knows the type. The things that make this kind of pilot a success in his "other" life are the same things that create problems whenever he sets foot in an airplane. Taking risks, challenging traditional lines of authority, bending an occasional rule, and pushing ahead when conditions aren't perfect can often separate the successful entrepreneur from the bankrupt dreamer—in business. In aviation, they can be the elements that lead the National Transportation Safety Board to determine that the probable cause of an accident was pilot error. For the controller who gets in the way, such personality traits can just as often mean a long, hard struggle with the executive pilot.

This was not the case, however, with the man who regularly flew left seat in King Air 1823 Bravo. In spite of his position and seemingly charmed life, he was in every respect a true gentleman. His skill in the air and his high regard for controllers were evident whenever he flew. On more than one occasion when he could have understandably become upset with less-than-perfect service, he instead happily tried to make the best of the situation we gave him. The closest he ever came to losing his eternal optimism was one night as he flew back home to Toledo, after what was probably a full day of business meetings.

For those of us in the radar room and just about every pilot in the Midwest, it had also been a long, tiring evening of extremely rough, unstable weather. For the better part of the day, a widespread area of intense thunderstorms had plagued aircraft operations in cities from Chicago to St. Louis. When the light green irregular blotches of rain began appearing along the western edges of our radarscopes, we prepared for the controlled chaos that was sure to follow.

As the thunderstorms moved closer and closer to the airport, activity inside and outside our little world increased. The radar site at the middle of the airport and all the communication and electronic equipment within the four walls around us were switched to backup generator power in case wind or lightning strikes interrupted our commercial power. The controllers in the tower began periodic updates on the sky condition and the severity of lightning as the storms became visible in the distance. On the radio frequencies, the familiar chatter of pilots wanting to know as much as possible about the storm movements steadily increased. Everyone who wasn't already busy soon would be.

The special requests from those in the air started coming in, one right after the other. Some pilots asked for radar vectors around the heaviest storm cells. Others wanted to hold in the air somewhere close to the airport until the squall line passed by. One or two wanted to try to beat the approaching weather to the runway. An F-100 fighter pilot returning from a practice mission, low on fuel, was one of those who decided to make an approach to the airport. When he was about six miles from the runway on final, I asked him how the ride had been so far.

"It's rougher than hell out here!" he said.

His report confirmed what we already strongly suspected. From time to time we would carefully pull back a corner of the blackout curtains in the radar room and steal a glance at the outside world. The ever-darkening sky put each of us on notice that the worst was far from over. Our work was just beginning.

During more serene days, pilots neither ask for nor want much more from controllers than that which is absolutely necessary. They just want to be kept safely separated from other airplanes and provided with the most direct, efficient means to their destinations. Anything more is seen as an intrusion into cockpits that rightfully belong only to the individuals flying. When the weather turns sour, a controller's input and judgment become a welcome and vital source of added information, unless the controller steps too far into the pilot's arena.

The F-100 succeeded in outrunning the storms. No sooner had the returning fighter touched down on runway 7 than a voice on the overhead speaker of the radar console called for my attention. A controller in Indianapolis Center had another inbound for me, King Air 1823 Bravo. The pilot knew about the storms that formed a barrier between himself and Toledo but believed he could thread his way safely through them.

When I first heard his familiar voice through my headset, it sounded as though the evening's weather had already taken its toll. His usual buoyant greeting was replaced with the words of another tired, overworked pilot who just wanted to get this last trip of the day over. An hour or two of dodging lightning, heavy rain, and rough air must have made him wonder whether or not getting home right away was worth the price he was paying. The last fifty miles would prove to be no easier than the previous several hundred had been.

He asked me if I would provide him with vectors around those areas of precipitation that looked heaviest on my radar. Between the assistance I could offer and his own airborne weather radar to confirm or deny my suggestions, he felt certain he could fly the final leg of his journey with a minimum of disruption or fuss.

We both went to work making the best of a crummy situation. I told 23 Bravo to descend to three thousand feet at his discretion, and he answered that it would be a long, slow descent. I suggested headings to fly around all but the lightest radar returns I was painting. About half of the time he agreed with my plans, and the other half he chose to fend for himself. By the time he zigged and zagged around those areas we had together determined were not at all conducive to safe flying, the last fifty miles turned out to be more like seventy-five or eighty.

When finally he got within range of our ILS (Instrument Landing System) approach to runway 7, there were no more major storms between him and the airport, but the battle was still far from being over. Severe turbulence continued to make his descent difficult. The King Air he was flying had, and still has, an unmatched reputation for performance and reliability, but when the sky turns into a giant roller coaster, even the best has to do everything a little slower. Otherwise the wings occasionally go where the rest of the airplane isn't.

By the time the pilot of 23 Bravo arrived at the point where his final descent to the runway should begin, our options were extremely limited. Those thunderstorms he had been skirting for the last twenty minutes were quickly closing in from all sides. He had only one way to go safely, and that was down toward the runway. I gave the pilot one last vector to intercept the final approach course, issued the appropriate, if superfluous, altitude restrictions, and cleared King Air 23 Bravo for the ILS runway 7 approach.

A little over ten more miles to fly and he would be on the runway. About six miles from touchdown, I asked the pilot to report his altitude. When he gave it to me, I began to have serious doubts about the outcome of his approach. I asked him if he could lose enough altitude in the limited space left. On other less hectic nights I had asked the same seemingly mindless question of countless other pilots. One of them, a United 727 captain, had answered in a deep, gravelly voice, "Oh I think so, son. In twenty-five years of flyin' I haven't left one up here yet."

The pilot in 23 Bravo, however, reacted to my question somewhat hostilely, apparently thinking my concern was instead a comment on his ability to fly the airplane. He said he was doing the very best that he could under the circumstances. He had been bouncing around all over the sky for the last two hours, he knew exactly where he was and how high he was, he fully intended to land at Toledo this time around, and if I thought I could do better I was welcome to try.

To say I was stunned doesn't really do justice to all that I was feeling at the moment. In almost four years of controlling traffic at Toledo, I had never once heard this man say anything harsh on the frequency. I felt as though I had just betrayed my best friend, and I didn't even know how.

Many times before and many times since, unreasonably irate pilots have been known to suffer the consequences of taking my sometimes short-lived patience beyond the limits of reasonable expectations. This time I wisely decided to keep my big mouth shut. It was my turn to answer, "Roger."

A couple of minutes later King Air 23 Bravo did in fact make a normal landing on runway 7, just as its pilot had said it would. I quietly sulked as I tended my severely wounded ego, and then I returned to my job of separating airplanes from airplanes and still other airplanes from weather. The heat of the battle soon passed, and I assumed all was quickly written off as an unfortunate misunderstanding.

Just about that time, the telephone on the supervisor's desk rang. He answered it, talked for a minute or two, and then yelled over to the front lines, "Who worked two three Bravo in?" As soon as my voice came back, I meekly answered, "Me." The supervisor, without saying another word, held the telephone receiver in the air for me. I felt all eyes in the radar room boring holes in me as I gingerly crawled toward the supervisor's desk. On the way over I silently rehearsed my new career: "Two double whoppers with cheese, a large order of fries, and a chocolate shake."

I took the receiver in hand. In spite of my better judgment, I asked the pilot what I could do for him. His answer was as much of a surprise to me as the first tirade had been. He wanted to apologize.

After landing, he had thought about our conversation on the frequency and realized my question wasn't meant to be the sarcastic remark he first took it to be. He went on to explain what we both already knew. It had been one of those nights when flying was more of a challenge than most of us cared to meet. I too apologized for unintentionally adding unnecessary headaches to his heavy work load, and we parted as friends.

Quite a few times after that night I worked King Air 1823 Bravo and its pilot through our airspace. Although specific mention of the events of that night was never again made by either one of us, I like to think we developed a mutual respect for each other's abilities and a common understanding of our shortcomings. I do know that every time since then, when he came on the frequency, he always made my day a little bit brighter.

RADAR CONTACT LOST

FOR ALMOST EVERY AIR TRAFFIC CONTROLLER, THERE IS ONE MEMORY that stays firmly implanted in the mind's consciousness. Never far from the surface, it's that one incident in which every detail, every moment, and every emotion can instantly be recalled in vivid detail, as though it happened yesterday. For me it happened on February 5, 1976. The airplane was Comanche 74 Papa.

Since the beginning of the day watch at 7:00 AM, conditions outside the radar room at Toledo Express Airport had changed very little. The official observer had been reporting the weather as indefinite ceiling two hundred, sky obscured, visibility one-half mile in moderate snow. Periodically throughout the day, runway 7 was closed just long enough for the snowplows and the sand trucks to make several runs up and down the length of it, and then it would again reopen for use. At best, the maintenance crews were barely keeping up with the steady snowfall. In spite of their efforts, the occasional inbound that did land at Toledo reported braking action on the runway as poor. It was possible to stop a couple of dozen tons of rolling airplane before it reached the end of the runway, but it was no picnic.

Conditions in the air weren't much better. ILS runway 7 was our approach in use, and all day long pilots on the approach had advised us they were on instruments, in the clouds, right down to minimums. They could finally see the runway and Mother Earth two hundred feet above the ground, just seconds before they landed. In some of the heavier snow squalls, only the "Rabbit" made landing possible. This fanciful name is given to the set of high-intensity strobe lights that align with the runway's centerline and illuminate the last half-mile of the approach. When the lights flash rapidly in sequence, they look like a rabbit running toward the runway, and pilots can "chase" them in for an accurate landing. Without the Rabbit to help pilots transition from instrument flight to looking out the cockpit windows, it would be on to another airport for more than one or two of them. Even with the Rabbit, this was a day for none but the most experienced aviators to be in the air.

Officially I was working the south sector arrival radar position. Unofficially it was known just as the south side. Unlike the airspace surrounding larger airports, which is divided into various wedges, corridors, and strata, places like Toledo normally have only two sectors. Instead of being a specialist who handles mainly arrivals, departures, or satellite operations, we drew a line down the middle of the airport. Inbound, outbound, overflying, or just hanging around, whatever airplanes appeared on the scopes north of that line, the north side handled. Whatever airplanes appeared south of that line, the south side worked. Unsatisfyingly simple for a government-inspired operation, but the system nevertheless worked rather well.

For the last hour and a half, I had been that south guy. Since the weather was so lousy, no airplane, no matter how large or small, could sneak through the cracks in the clouds and land at the airport without first talking to me. In truth, I had been sitting there for about an hour and a half, but it would be difficult to describe the majority of what I did there as work. Without all the FLIBS (which affectionately stands for fucking little itinerant bastards— those VFR [visual flight rules] pilots who sometimes wander aimlessly around the sky just enjoying the pure pleasure of flight), our traffic had been exceedingly light all day.

The bulk of our attention was concentrated toward the clock on the wall and the door to the radar room. Soon the afternoon crew should come walking in, and after spending a few minutes briefing my relief on what was happening and what might happen,

I would be on my way home. As I was turning my thoughts to things other than airplanes, a concerned voice came to me through my headset.

The controller working local in the tower was talking: "You're not going to believe this. Look in the vicinity of the Waterville VOR." My eyes immediately began searching an area eleven miles south-southeast of the airport. There, a little circle electronically superimposed on the scope designated the navigational aid known as Waterville VOR (VHF omnidirectional range). Its counterpart on the ground, a small, white block building with what looked like a large, white, upside-down ice-cream cone on its roof, is one of the reasons pilots can accurately navigate through the clouds. The 360 degrees of radio signals it continuously transmits into the air, when coupled with similar signals from another VOR eighty or a hundred miles away, make up the airways that instrument pilots use to stay on course. Over the years, pilots flying visually have also learned to depend on this easier and more precise means of navigation, especially when the weather isn't exactly terrific.

Local went on to say that in the vicinity of Waterville VOR a 74 Papa, inbound to Toledo, would be calling me. He was flying VFR, using only outside reference to the ground and to make matters worse, he was running low on fuel. Thinking that was more than enough to make the next few minutes interesting, I acknowledged him with "Roger."

"Now he says he's running out of fuel and is being forced down by icing! I'm putting him on your frequency," Local said.

My first instinct was to laugh. It was all just a bit too much and had to be a joke created by a couple of extremely bored controllers in the tower. It wouldn't be the first time a controller in the radar room was called by a nonexistent pilot, from the standby radio in the tower.

What makes this deception possible is a blue box, the battery-operated backup transceiver. It's intended to be used in the unlikely event (a euphemism for watch out, because sooner or later I guarantee you'll need it) that there is a complete failure of our communication equipment. With the blue box, we could still talk to the pilots—if not all of them, then at least some of them, which is, after all, better than nothing.

When the emergency radio isn't being used by a controller to salvage what might seem like a hopeless, out-of-control situation, it can conveniently be used to contact another controller. With just the slightest bit of imagination and a disguised voice, the person instigating the call can go on for several minutes, acting like the world's dumbest pilot. Eventually, of course, the other controller catches on. Eventually.

As the troubled pilot was supposedly being switched to my frequency, I envisioned another controller in the tower muffling the microphone with a handkerchief and calling me in a stilted German accent: "Hello Toledo Approach, this iss Fokker seven four Papa, ofer." The whole ordeal would have been just the thing to ease the boredom of the day. Except that when I looked at my scope in the direction of Waterville VOR, there was a faint, slow-moving primary target inching its way indirectly toward Toledo.

The pilot of 74 Papa finally called me, and exactly what he said was almost too much for me to comprehend. He reported just passing Waterville VOR, and he again mentioned that he was low on fuel. His heading indicator—the one instrument that provides precise directional guidance—wasn't working quite right, and finally, he wanted assistance getting into Toledo Express. Oh, and one more thing. He was flying VFR, and snow and low clouds were making that more and more difficult.

The only bright spot in the entire conversation so far had been that the pilot was incredibly calm, or so he sounded. Being about midway in my own instrument training, I could only mutter under my breath, "I'm glad it's you and not me out there!" It was all I could do to maintain an air of nonchalance in the midst of a situation that was quickly going from bad to downright ugly. Someone with a little less sensitivity to the problem yelled from the other end of the room, "Hey, what do you want? This is why we get the big bucks!"

I reaffirmed Comanche 74 Papa's position, gave the pilot the current official weather at Toledo, and asked if he was IFR-rated, qualified for instrument flight in the clouds. For some reason I had long since forgotten, a controller was never supposed to ask that last question. But as one who occasionally bent the rules to fit the variations that frequently cropped up, I wasn't terribly concerned. When the pilot answered yes, I asked him if he would like to file an IFR flight plan into Toledo. He replied, "Affirmative." Maybe this wasn't going to be so bad after all.

I issued 74 Papa a clearance and said, "Comanche seven four Papa, climb and maintain two thousand five hundred. Fly heading three one zero vectors for the ILS runway seven final approach course." Almost as an afterthought, I asked the pilot if he had enough fuel to turn about a seven-mile final. He unexpectedly but emphatically answered, "Negative!" That meant a couple of things. First, it meant the Comanche didn't have enough fuel to stay in the air another fifteen or twenty minutes. More important, it meant the pilot most likely didn't really have any idea how long he could stay airborne.

General aviation airplanes have become remarkably reliable machines, but one area in which there has been little or no progress is with the gauges that indicate how much fuel is left in the tanks. With most light airplanes, when the needles go below a quarter of a tank, it's anybody's guess how much fuel is really there to use.

Since the weather was so bad, I was legally required to vector any pilot wanting to fly the ILS to a position at least two miles outside the outer marker. The outer marker is an electronic signal device located five miles from the approach end of the runway. As a pilot flies over it, a receiver in the airplane emits a loud beep, alerting the pilot to begin the final descent to the runway. Hence the seven-mile final needed to make 74 Papa's approach to the airport legal. Of course, "legal" wouldn't mean a whole lot if the Comanche quit flying before the runway appeared.

I then told the pilot that I could give him a surveillance approach to runway 7 with a close turn on. During a surveillance approach, or ASR (airport surveillance radar), I would verbally provide the pilot with all the information he needed to fly his airplane right down to the runway. Instead of using the localizer signal on the ILS system to line him up with the runway centerline, I would use my radarscope to guide the pilot precisely to the runway. With a magnified version of my normal radar display, I would watch the primary radar target as it moved closer to the runway, issuing turns, distance information, and suggested altitudes to the pilot. That left the pilot free to concentrate solely on flying the airplane while listening to my directions.

I could also modify the length of the final approach course, since I was, in essence, providing the course guidance with my vectors. The final could be as short as one mile or as long as fifteen, depending upon the circumstances. Given the weather conditions, I suggested a three-mile final and the pilot agreed. That would save the pilot about eight or nine miles of flying and probably four or five minutes. At the time, those few minutes didn't seem like much, but it was the best I could offer. Runway 7 was the only runway with approach lights, the Rabbit, and high-intensity runway lights. Without them it seemed doubtful that the pilot would ever see the runway.

Even with all the lights, the ASR approach had some serious drawbacks. Foremost was the weather. Technically, pilots on an ASR approach can fly no lower than four hundred feet above the runway unless they have the runway in sight. All day long, no one had seen the runway much higher than two hundred feet above it. If Comanche 74 Papa was going to land, he would have to descend illegally below the published minimums for the approach. He knew it, and I knew I was setting us both up for disciplinary action when it was all over. Although I didn't like it at all, I could think of no other reasonable alternative. What I really wanted was for anyone but me to be sitting there making those decisions.

It seemed a good time to ask the pilot if he wanted to declare an emergency. That would give both of us the authority to ignore any and all regulations as necessary to achieve the successful culmination of an otherwise dubious flight. His answer, "Not yet."

Here was a pilot who had been slightly lost while flying visually during one of the worst snowstorms of the season. Some essential equipment wasn't working quite right, the outcome of the approach he was going to make was highly questionable, and he was almost out of fuel. But he wanted to wait a little while longer to see what else developed before going out on a limb and declaring an emergency. Somehow, it didn't come as much of a surprise that the wait wasn't too terribly long.

"Ah, Approach, Comanche seven four Papa. My compass is leaking fluid and it's giving me fits. I don't know how much longer I can keep this thing in the air."

What little ability the pilot had had to fly specific headings, or stay headed in one direction as opposed to any other, was gone. My role in this unraveling debacle was increasing with each minute, and I was beginning to like it less and less. In a last-ditch effort to save myself from a multimillion-dollar lawsuit, I declared an emergency for the pilot. Practically speaking, my declaration would make no difference to the outcome. Everyone was already doing as much as they possibly could. I just wanted to go on record as having said this whole thing just wasn't kosher.

Over the years, as regulations have become more complex, lawsuits more frequent, sums of money sought more exorbitant, and FAA enforcement policies more harsh, pilots have become less and less inclined to declare emergencies. Pilots and controllers have become increasingly concerned about possible legal implications instead of focusing on how to prevent serious accidents. Evidently the pilot of Comanche 74 Papa was no different.

I told the pilot that his surveillance approach would now be a no-gyro approach to runway 7. The no-gyro approach meant that I would literally tell the pilot when to start a turn and when to stop a turn instead of giving him compass headings to fly. Based on the track his target made as it moved across my radarscope, I would time how long I wanted the pilot to stay in a turn. Though not as precise as an ASR approach, with the no-gyro approach I should be able little by little to line up the Comanche with the runway.

Again the pilot expressed concern about the length of time he could keep his airplane flying, and for the first time I sensed fear in his voice. There was only one more trick in the bag, but it would push me a little farther out on the limb I was already hanging on to for dear life. At this point I also knew I didn't have much more to lose, but the same wasn't true for the pilot and his passenger. I told the pilot what the wind was doing, stiffly blowing out of the northeast, and asked him if he wanted a no-gyro to runway 34 instead of 7. The good news was that runway 34 was only eight miles away instead of the twenty or more miles he would have to fly to runway 7. The bad news was that the wind and the lack of approach lights on runway 34 would test both his ability and mine to the limits. It was his choice.

Wisely, I think, the pilot opted for the approach to runway 34. Having already flown a mile or so beyond the extended centerline of the runway, the Comanche had to be momentarily turned back to the northeast, repositioned, turned to the northwest, and then aimed directly at the airport. We both knew that his approach had to be continued until the pilot was directly over the runway. There just wasn't enough time for anything else. Although I would have to fudge a little and guess a little, I felt I had about a 95 percent chance of giving the pilot an accurate estimate of his arrival at the beginning edge of the runway. I knew too that the controllers in the tower would be straining to catch even a glimpse of the Comanche as it approached, and their last-minute instructions could be just enough to save the day.

At four miles everything looked unexpectedly good. The Comanche was almost perfectly lined up with the runway, and the indication was that, in spite of the strong wind blowing the airplane sideways, the pilot was doing an excellent job of staying on course. From a couple of chairs down the line I heard Leo yell out, "Hey, Van, it looks like you've got yourself a save!"

A save is official recognition from the FAA that a controller or a flight service specialist was able to successfully assist a pilot in distress. There are hundreds of official saves recorded each year and easily just as many that never get written down. Most often they involve pilots who find themselves lost, sometimes temporarily, sometimes hopelessly. Occasionally more extensive services are provided. Either way, being involved in a save is truly one of the very best parts of being an air traffic controller. Official or not, being there when someone needs help and being able to provide it leaves you with an incredibly warm feeling inside. At the moment I wasn't quite ready to feel relieved or good, but I started to believe the pilot could pull this one off.

At two and a half miles from the runway, I noticed that the Comanche was heading right of the course. I told the pilot to begin a turn to the left. He answered something, but it was just garbled enough for his comment to be unintelligible. At two miles, Comanche 74 Papa suddenly and unexpectedly vanished from my radarscope. I tried contacting the pilot on the radio. Then I tried again, and once more. I quickly called the controllers in the tower to ask if they had seen anything at all outside. The snow made it impossible to see even the approach end of the runway, and although they had tried and tried, they saw nothing.

Two miles. Another sixty or seventy seconds and Comanche 74 Papa might have been on the runway, but it didn't happen. The last transmission I made was one final statement for the lawyers in the front office, just so there was no mistaking what happened: "Comanche seven four Papa, radar contact lost two miles southeast of Toledo Express Airport."

From the time the tower controller first alerted me to the plight of the people in 74 Papa to my last transmission, eight minutes had elapsed. Not a terribly long time to decide anyone's fate, except that it was one long minute too long. Seconds later, a terribly sick feeling erupted within me. The first clear thought that surfaced was that my best had not been good enough. With it came the frightening reality that there would be no save recorded, and try as I might I could do nothing else. I had just lost an airplane, and I was at least partially responsible for the people who had been inside it.

TAPES DON'T LIE

SIX MINUTES AFTER 74 PAPA DISAPPEARED FROM MY RADARSCOPE, I was officially relieved from working arrival south. The police and rescue crews had already been dispatched to the general vicinity of the accident, and although we didn't know the exact location of the crash site, the search area wasn't very large. We were reasonably certain that we would know the fate of the occupants within a few minutes.

For me, I suspect some level of shock had finally begun to materialize. Up to the moment when I realized that 74 Papa was not going to make it to the airport, I remember the details vividly. After that moment, I can recall absolutely nothing of what I did or thought or felt until I arrived in the training room to listen to the tape recording of our conversation. Then my first recollection is a phone call to my wife, telling her I would not be home at the expected time. I told her nothing except that some problems at work needed to be resolved before I could leave. Thinking back, I know my reason for not telling her what had happened was not my desire not to worry her; rather, I just couldn't bring myself to admit to being a part of the accident.

As with any accident, the controller or controllers involved have little or no time to reflect on what went wrong. The normal course of events is to give the supervisor and tower chief a quick synopsis, listen to the tapes, and write a narrative statement describing the controller's, and thereby the FAA's, side of the story. Since any and all of what a controller says, does, and writes can and frequently is used later in the courts, anyone involved in an incident or accident was supposed to have the benefit of a union representative throughout the entire proceedings.

PATCO had long since determined that, when it came time to place the blame on someone, exoneration of the individual controller and exoneration of the FAA and the rest of its representatives were not necessarily one and the same. In many respects, people ended up watching out for themselves. The union representative was there to make sure that an "inadvertent" omission didn't put the controller in a position more tenuous than that which already existed.

For whatever reason, my protector was nowhere to be found during those initial critical hours immediately following the accident. I was, however, new enough to the FAA that I naively thought all those management and labor precautions were overkill anyway. I fully trusted the people responsible for my welfare. I had done the very best I could do, and I had to believe that the front office would now do the same for me. Although I quickly began to get a sense that my ideas might be slightly askew, not until many years later in Pittsburgh would I fully realize how wrong I had been. There was undoubtedly a higher source watching over me, but he didn't get a paycheck from the FAA.

For the first time, as I sat in the stark, windowless confines of our training room waiting for the tapes to be brought to me, my mind began to play terrible tricks. With still no word from the crash site, I asked myself if they would find victims or survivors. If it turned out they were the former, would it be my fault? Then the "what-ifs" started to flow. What if I had suggested an ASR to runway 34 in the beginning; would the Comanche have had enough fuel to get to the runway? What if I hadn't told the pilot to climb to 2,500 feet before I started vectoring him to the airport; would the fuel wasted in the climb have been enough to prevent the crash?

At the moment, it mattered little that the solutions I was proposing to myself were valid only because I now possessed information I didn't have before. Based on what I learned after the accident, I had in fact made the wrong decisions. Based on what I knew at the time, my reactions were most probably the right ones. Had I not climbed the pilot to 2,500 feet he might have had enough fuel to make it to the runway, but he also might have hit a tower, a building, or some other obstruction along the way. Still, as I sat at the cold, gray metal, government-issue table playing my intellect against my emotions, I started to feel more and more like the criminal sitting in what could easily have been the interrogation room at the local precinct.

The longer I sat there alone, thinking, the harder it became to absolve myself of any guilt. Finally the tape recording arrived, and with it the first word from the rescue team. By the time the team had arrived at the downed airplane, no one was there. All they found was the Comanche, still reasonably intact. Inside, blood was spattered on the instrument panel, but no people were to be found. Someone apparently saw the crippled plane land and had taken the pilot and his passenger somewhere for medical treatment.

Although that first report by no means relieved me of my feelings of responsibility, it brightened my hopes considerably. The only saving grace of the whole situation was that the accident was caused as a result of fuel starvation. Because there was no fuel in the plane when it went down, there was also nothing to ignite on impact. With most crashes, it isn't the abrupt contact with the ground that kills its victims. It isn't even the heat or the fire that result when the highly volatile aviation fuel bursts into flames. Dense toxic smoke is the reason most people die in airplane crashes. Since Comanche 74 Papa didn't have any fuel, there was no fire. If the passengers inside were wearing their seat belts, there was a very good chance that both of them could have escaped without serious injuries. That was the thought I tried to keep running through my mind as I first listened to the recording of our conversations on the frequency.

At least twice a year controllers are required, and in my case physically forced, to listen to recordings of themselves talking to pilots on the frequencies. The thinking is that, if a picture is worth a thousand words, then a recording complete with all the uhs, stuttering, and corrections is worth at least ten times that amount. Usually it is. Most controllers after ten or fifteen minutes of listening to themselves tend to blurt out something like, "That babbling buffoon on the tape can't possibly be me. There must be some mistake." Except there is no mistake. One man's *cool* is another man's *crummy*.

Listening to a conversation that might include someone's last words and responses of mine that I already believed were wrong only made the whole exercise much more painful. Since in the last hour I had been reminded several times that I needed to write a statement, I had no choice in the matter. I listened, not once but several times, to the saga of Comanche 74 Papa.

On several different counts, I needed to satisfy my curiosity. At least twice toward the end of his flight, the pilot had made brief comments that were so quick and garbled I didn't understand what he was saying. Replaying the tape two or three times would give me the chance to find out whether I had missed something that might have changed the outcome.

When I finally figured out his first mumbled comment, I was stunned. He had said, "Fuel just ran out." His second and, now I realized, his last words were just as discomforting as the first. In a voice almost completely devoid of emotion, he said, "We're not going to make it." As I sat in front of the playback machine, straining my ears to be certain I had not misunderstood the clipped phrases for a second time, a couple of different thoughts came to mind. The transmission had said all there was to say. Although I sensed a faint plea for help in the pilot's tone, that could have been my mind playing tricks. It was extremely unsettling, but I don't know what I could have said in response. Any words would have been sorely inadequate. Selfishly, I was glad that my requests for a repeat had gone unanswered.

By now, others too had listened to the tape. An investigative team would soon be dispatched to the crash site, and Washington would want all the mounds of paperwork generated by such an accident sent in as soon as possible. In spite of the fact that everyone who stopped to see me in the training room repeatedly said I had done all the right things, I began to sense that I would receive the full support of the FAA only when, and if, my potential guilt was completely erased. The first copy of the written statement that was brought to me for a signature only increased my uneasiness.

My written statement was to be my recollection of the events that had transpired. Listening to the tapes was supposed to refresh my mind in an atmosphere more conducive to objectivity. But when it came time for writing, only those things I did, heard, or said at the time the events were taking place should have been included. When the first official copy of the statement was given to me for inspection, the two last comments the pilot made were added in, without my responses asking him to repeat them. The result was an official document stating that the pilot in trouble told the controller he was going down and the controller, in this case me, ignored the information and went on with business as usual. I felt bad enough about the whole thing once I listened to the tape and realized what I had missed. Having it included in a statement—incorrectly, I thought—only made matters worse. The statement was rewritten with the changes I requested. I signed it, and into the official accident package it went.

By the time an hour or so had gone by, my role in the investigation was just about over, at least for the time being. Still others kept coming into the training room, and every time the door opened, my stomach tightened. I presumed I was about to find out how the pilot and his passenger were doing. But no one knew where they had been taken or even whether they were alive or dead, so my own tension and punishment kept lingering on.

Just before I was ready to leave, Dave, our deputy chief, came in to go over the accident and my role in it one more time. Having listened to the tape, listened to my story, and discussed it with the rest of the staff, he felt I had done almost everything by the book. There was just one problem that might come back to bite me. When I gave Comanche 74 Papa an IFR clearance, I had failed to ask the pilot his altitude. If the airplane was at an altitude higher than eight thousand feet, the top of our airspace, then I had illegally issued a clearance in Cleveland Center's airspace. And as he said it, I felt the noose begin to tighten.

Technically, he was correct. If the airplane was high, Cleveland Center easily could have had another airplane in that vicinity, and my clearance could have created the potential for a midair collision. But to my thinking, logically that would have been a faulty assumption. All day long, pilots flying in the area where 74 Papa first appeared had been reporting solid clouds up to at least twenty or twenty-five thousand feet. Pilots foolish enough to try flying VFR on a day like that usually did it by "scud running."

Scud running is flying by visual reference to the ground in

weather that is far less than ideal. While scud running isn't exactly illegal, it's usually unsafe. VFR pilots who do it tend to follow highways, railroad tracks, or some other prominent landmarks so they can keep track of where they are. Problems of scud running include obstructions that are higher than the airplane is flying and the possibility that other airplanes are doing the same thing but flying in the opposite direction. Because of the poor flight visibility that usually encourages scud running, these unexpected obstacles to flight can pop up out of nowhere right in front of an unsuspecting pilot. When they do, the pilot is most often the loser.

I had assumed that 74 Papa was not above the clouds but was instead flying low enough to the ground to see it. It seemed to me that the end result tended to support my position. In a little less than eight minutes, the pilot had reached the ground—a descent not easily accomplished if he had been above eight thousand feet to begin with—and when I advised him to climb to 2,500 feet, he should have told me if other than a climb was necessary. In spite of everything, I began to feel more and more responsible, but for exactly what I didn't know.

Our deputy chief said there was nothing more I could do at the airport. I had done a good job and I wasn't to worry about anything. Easy to say, not so easy to do. But with still no word on either the pilot or his passenger, there was little else for me to do but go home. The deputy chief assured me that as soon as they had any word on their condition he would call me.

The truth was that I needed to go home but I wasn't ready to leave the airport. I didn't want to be alone with my thoughts, and as much as I wanted someone's company, I knew my wife couldn't really understand how I was feeling. Only my colleagues at work knew what it felt like to be caught up in the midst of someone else's struggle for survival. No matter who tried to help, deep down I knew that only if the two people from 74 Papa were safe would I really feel any better.

The drive home was alternately filled with agony and peacefulness, ironically for the same reason. It was agony because I knew the answer to my only important question wouldn't come in the car, and it was peaceful for the very same reason. The snow, now falling heavily, seemed to insulate me from the real world outside. In truth, I didn't want the ride home to end. I just wanted to continue hoping for the best without having to know the answers.

Like a script for a poorly imagined movie, my answer came as I pulled in the driveway. A news bulletin interrupted the local radio program to announce that earlier in the evening a light plane had crashed while attempting an emergency landing at Toledo Express Airport. The two occupants of the aircraft had survived the crash and were being treated for injuries at St. Luke's Hospital in Maumee, Ohio.

I knew the emotional strain of the past couple of hours had been great for a few of us, but I didn't have any idea how high it had been for me until I heard that broadcast. As I sat in the driveway with the engine and lights off, silently watching the snow melting as it fell on the windshield, a chill started at the back of my neck and with almost lightning speed traveled the entire length and depth of my body. When it was over, tears started to fall from my eyes, and hard as I tried, for the next few minutes nothing I could do would stop them. No matter what might come back to haunt me in the days ahead, when I finally got out of the car to go inside, I had left the worst behind me.

Strangely enough, other than the comments and questions I received the first two or three days after the accident, nothing about 74 Papa or its two people ever came up officially. I never learned the names of the people involved, never read the accident report, and actually never even knew if there was one. I could only guess that the actions I took as a result of the pilot's requests were never called into question. Thirteen years later, the only tangible memory I have of the accident is the piece of yellowing copy paper on which I wrote my statement that night in 1976.

My involvement with the lives of those two strangers might have affected decisions I made in the years that followed, but I doubt I will ever know how much. I know I feel a tremendous empathy for anyone involved in a situation where loss of life is the result, and I know the feeling of helplessness that overwhelms them. Moreover, thirteen years later I can still hear the Comanche pilot's voice when he said, "We're not going to make it." But once in a while, if the memory happened to crop up while I was working, even that was too much to remember.

WRONG SIDE OF THE FENCE

MINNEAPOLIS. IT WASN'T ATLANTA OR O'HARE (and if there were any doubts, all I had to do was ask one of the ex–O'Hare controllers who came to Minneapolis to retire), but for an inexperienced rookie from Toledo it was still the big time. Toledo had five or six gates, and about the only time they were all full was after ten o'clock at night when the overnighters came home to roost. Minneapolis Wold Chamberlain Airport had fifty-six, and more often than not most of them were occupied.

Minneapolis was home base for Northwest Airlines and North Central Airlines, which later became Republic which later became Northwest. Add to that a bunch of airplanes belonging to Western, Braniff, USAir, Eastern, and all the local commuters, and there was the potential for a big airport. What made it even better was that Minneapolis also happened to be the location where the original *Airport* was filmed. Downstairs in the controller's breakroom was an aging stereo console, the kind made of light Scandinavian wood with little spindly legs that had metal protectors on the ends. It was covered with scuff marks and scratches, but down in one corner was a small brass plaque that read, "With appreciation from the cast and crew of Airport."

All mine were the tower and radar room that millions of

movie fans had viewed as the crippled 707 struggled to make it home. As I stood in the tower and looked out across runway 22 to the terminal building on the other side of the field, at least for the moment, pride in what I was about to become overwhelmed my fears. Hundreds of people would soon be depending upon me to get them safely along that first leg of the journey. Though the distance from even the farthest gate to any runway was little more than a mile and a half, it was an important part of the trip. Some of the world's worst airplane disasters had happened on the ground before takeoff or shortly after landing.

I quickly learned that the size of the airport and the number of airplanes it handled weren't the only things that were different in Minneapolis. The controllers in general and my crew in particular were tough. In Toledo when pilots made mistakes, most of the time we tried to help turn them into learning experiences. In Minneapolis if pilots screwed up, the people on our side of the field chewed them up and down.

One day as I watched a slight, wiry controller colleague named Vern working ground control, I found out just how sardonic controllers could be. Ever since the well-known airplane hijacking incidents, airport security had become a top priority for both the FAA and local governments. Minneapolis was no different. The airport police and the airport management took great pride in having a secure establishment, and anyone who threatened it was sure to end up in serious trouble, if not in jail. I suspect the two youngsters who jumped the security fence for a closer look at the airplanes had no idea what the consequences could be.

As is the case with almost every ground control position at a major airport, when one airplane starts to move out of the gate, within minutes the rest invariably follow. Vern was more than busy trying to get pilots where they wanted to go as soon as they wanted to go there when the call from airport security came through on the ground control frequency.

"Ah, Ground, this is airport security. You got a minute?"

Vern's reply was, "Hell no, I don't got a minute! I'm up to my ass in airplanes!" Then he keyed his microphone so his next reply would be the one that went out on the frequency, and in a businesslike tone he answered, "Affirmative, Security, what do you need?"

"We apprehended a couple of kids who must've jumped the

perimeter fence and violated security. What do you want us to do with them?"

Vern turned toward the rest of us in the tower cab and repeated what he had just received through his headset. In spite of all the things controllers at large airports are responsible for, the disposal of errant juvenile delinquents was never part of the position description.

As I found out about a year later, Vern was a quiet man of very few words, but the ones he chose to speak could be painfully concise. By then I was working arrival handoff in the radar room, and I became one of Vern's victims. The arrival handoff controller is important for a couple of reasons, not the least of which is to ensure that the arrival controller never gets more airplanes than can be safely fit into a rather confined piece of airspace. The handoff controller talks on the landline intercom to those controllers who talk to the pilots just before they fly across the imaginary line that delineates the Minneapolis Approach Control airspace. In this instance, those controllers were the enroute controllers in Minneapolis Center.

The center controllers would take the airplanes that departed from Chicago, Atlanta, Las Vegas, or wherever and carefully jockey them around the sky so that as they arrived in our airspace they would be slowed down to 250 knots and arranged in a neat line, one behind the other, no closer than five miles a part. If traffic got really heavy, the center controllers would get on the handoff line and start making deals with arrival handoff.

"Hey Approach, can you buy Northwest at ten and Braniff at eleven? Chicago gave them to me late, high, and fast." Or maybe it would be, "Approach, USAir was off the frequency talking to company. Can you take her side by side with Northwest and work it out in your airspace?"

As often as possible, the arrival handoff controller would take as much as the arrival controller could safely handle. After all, when all those airplanes that had arrived at once started departing at the same time, it would be our turn to ask the center to buy a few deals here and there. The official procedures may have looked good on paper, but when the airplanes started moving, it was cooperation between the controllers on the frontlines that made it all work out.

This particular day, Vern was working arrival control combined on a runway 4 operation. For some reason, Vern was doing alone what two controllers normally would share. To add to the complexity, a runway 4 operation meant there was only one runway available for arrivals instead of the two parallel runways we preferred to use. Half the normal runway capacity didn't mean only half the usual number of airplanes came to Minneapolis. It meant that the controllers spent more time delaying them in the air until there were slots available for landing.

Two other factors increased the already heavy burden on Vern. Runway 4 location meant that the majority of our arrivals, which came in over the southern arrival fixes, would have a shorter distance to the airport and would be with us in no time at all. Vern either had to already have a spot selected for each inbound or have someplace else in which to delay the airplanes. If the number of inbounds became just too many for the airspace, the handoff controller could tell the center to shut them off. No more arrivals would be accepted until order was restored for those already in the area. The problem was, I was the handoff man. I was supposed to make that decision long before things got out of hand, and I was new to the position.

As I had already discovered on more than one occasion, being legally certified to work a control position wasn't the same as being qualified to do it. I quickly found out there was a lot of truth to the saying "When the training ends, the real learning begins." Unfortunately for both Vern and me, I was somewhere between the end of that training and the beginning of learning. As for the controllers in Minneapolis Center they must have loved me. Whatever they wanted I approved.

Little by little, Vern got busier and busier. Being the good controller that he was, he kept increasing the pace of his words but never changed the level and tone. I figured as long as he sounded good I must be doing everything right, except there seemed to be an awful lot of airplanes concentrated in one sector of our airspace, his.

Finally, in that same even, undisturbed tone of voice, Vern turned his head ever so slightly away from the mass of airplanes on the radarscope, looked me in the eyes, and quietly said, "Van, if you want to kill me that badly, why don't you just cut my heart out and get it over with."

Slowly the light dawned on me. It was time to tell the center to spread out the rest of the inbounds. Vern never said another word to me or anyone else, even though he had more than enough reason to.

And the errant youths who jumped the fence? They were spread-eagled against the airport police car, just in case they were the advance wave of insurgents sent to cripple our nation's air transportation system. They knew nothing of Vern nor of his totally unique sense of humor. All they heard was Vern's reply to security's question, "What do you want us to do with them?"

In the tower, he had paused only momentarily before keying the microphone. Then, in a tone that indicated nothing but business, he said only two words to the waiting police officer: "Waste 'em!"

Almost immediately, he banged his forehead with the open palm of his hand and yelled at himself, "Jesus Christ! What if those crazy cops think I'm serious." Fortunately for more than just Vern, the cops weren't as crazy as he might have thought, and they took no immediate action to carry out his execution order. But I imagine that those two kids never again entertained the idea of scaling our fence or any other one.

Only one other time did I witness a serious breach of security while working in Minneapolis, and its innocent beginnings did little to compensate for the momentary terror it created before it was all over. I was the ground controller when I noticed an unknown automobile roaming aimlessly around on the taxiways adjacent to the main parking ramp of the airport. It caught my attention for a couple of reasons. One, it was a car I had never seen before, and while occasionally politicians, surveyors, construction supervisors, or other invited guests examined various portions of the airport, we always had been notified of their presence in advance. Two, this nondescript vehicle devoid of any markings, official or otherwise, had just entered what was known in official FAA language as the movement area.

On one side of the demarcation line, in the nonmovement area—a misnomer in itself since constant and occasionally frenzied movement of vehicles and airplanes was always occurring but without FAA guidance—anything was permissible. As the "ramp rats" scurried around from one airplane to another loading or unloading baggage, refueling empty wing tanks, pushing or pulling wide-body jets hundreds of times their size, near misses and even rare collisions were a matter of course. As long as whatever happened happened in the nonmovement area outside of the purview of the feds, neither the FAA nor its representatives, the controllers, wanted to know about it. In fact, the less they knew about what went on, the better they liked it. That way, when the captain of a multimillion-dollar 747 just moving out of the gate asked ground control if he was aware that a truck carrying the latest discharge from another plane's johns almost wiped out his nosewheel, the ground controller could respond, "Sorry, sir, but I'm not responsible for that area of the ramp."

If, however, the same thing occurred on the other side of the boundary, it was an entirely different matter. Designated portions of the ramp, all taxiways, and all runways were considered movement area. Anything or anyone who wanted to move here had to have first received the appropriate authorization from someone in the tower. The unmarked brown car driving around on my taxiway didn't have that authorization. So far it was only a minor irritation, but if anything happened it was going to be my head on the block.

I started transmitting in the blind: "Brown vehicle on the taxiway abeam the tower, state your identification and intentions please." No answer.

Repeated calls with all the authority I could muster yielded nothing more. The plain brown car crept along the taxiway, getting closer and closer to runway 29R, one of our main arrival runways. As much as I hated to do it, I had to tell the controller working local that there was a vehicle moving toward the runway and that I didn't have the situation under complete control.

Local control answered, "I don't care how you do it, but you'd better keep that son of a bitch off my runway!"

I called airport security, told them the problem, and asked if they would find out who was driving the car and why he was on the taxiways without a clearance. Unfortunately I was just a couple of minutes too late.

As our wandering gypsy neared the intersection of the taxiway and the runway I warned local that soon there might be an unexpected visitor on the runway. At the same time I looked out toward the approach end of the runway to see if the car would cause any problems for the arrivals. My heart gave me the answer as it worked its way out of my chest and continued up past my vocal cords. Just about to touch down on the pavement less than two miles away was a nice shiny Eastern DC-9.

The local controller was at least two steps ahead of me. He had forewarned the pilot of the DC-9 that the automobile on the taxiway two-thirds of the way down the runway was both unauthorized to be there and uncontrollable. The pilot answered that he had the car in sight and would be able to stop long before he arrived at that intersection. But, he added, he would pay very close attention to its movement.

As the nosewheel of the DC-9 planted itself firmly on the runway, committing pilots and passengers to a landing, the driver of the old brown car started across the runway with the precision of a high-priced stunt driver. We in the tower could do little but watch and hope that the Eastern captain was true to his word and that the crazy driver whoever he was, wouldn't do something even crazier.

For a split second the car started to turn toward the DC-9 rolling out on the runway, and then just as quickly it turned away and continued across the runway. For the next five or ten minutes, all the runways at Minneapolis became a tactical battleground for the unknown intruder and three airport police cars. As the chase continued from one runway to another, all the airplane traffic into or out of Minneapolis came to a halt. Inbounds were being held in the skies around the Twin Cities and departures were being held at their respective gates until the mad runway crasher was cornered or disabled. Although he had never came within striking distance of the Eastern DC-9, everyone involved decided that one try was more than enough.

After a few more minutes of deft maneuvering by both the fugitive and our local authorities, the chase ended. The brown sedan and its driver had been cornered at the approach end of runway 11L, less than a mile away from where it had all begun. Carefully the three police officers emerged from their cars with weapons drawn. Just as carefully they tightened the circle they had formed around the suspect vehicle. Evidently, seeing that he was trapped with nowhere to run, the criminal opened the door of the brown sedan and stepped out. With everyone in the tower fighting for the two pairs of binoculars to see first hand what this maniac looked like, none of us got a really good look at him. But from what we could see, maniac didn't quite fit the bill. In fact, the driver more closely resembled someone's gray-haired grandfather.

It turned out that's just what he was. After dropping his wife off at the terminal building, the man had driven toward what he thought was the airport parking lot. But he had followed closely on the heels of a food truck as it moved through the security gate onto the main ramp. Once he found himself on the other side of the world, everything became more and more confusing. Finally, the sight of the DC-9 closing in on him made his mistake all too apparent. And still he could find no way to somehow get himself back through the looking glass.

When he realized that the three cars following him around the airport weren't three other lost souls trying to get to safety, he was only too glad to allow himself to be cornered. Badly shaken, terribly apologetic, and just plain happy to have been rescued, the little man in the brown sedan was led back through the gate into his own safe world. We in the tower spent much of the rest of the day trying to imagine how big a DC-9 must look as it's seen through the windshield of a 1965 Plymouth.

HEAVY TRAFFIC AND HEAVY HANDS

MINNEAPOLIS TURNED OUT TO BE A LOT OF OTHER THINGS BESIDES a place where strange and unusual events occasionally happened. It was a place where I learned a lot and a place where I grew up. Sometimes I was filled with the exhilaration of accomplishing a task that only days before had seemed impossible. Sometimes I was filled with the pain of learning that the world of the "big time" wasn't always the most pleasant place to be. But even when the bad seemed to outweigh the good, there were always one or two people who helped to even the score.

One of those people was Dick. Dick was short and stocky, with a powerfully built frame and an outspoken manner. He was seldom challenged by anyone, and I quickly understood that his nickname was well chosen and well deserved. Anytime anyone yelled for "Animal," Dick would answer with a low guttural growl that left no doubt he was the person being addressed. The only person who exercised any control over him was Mrs. Animal, Anne, and in spite of what he might say, we knew that she knew exactly what she was doing.

Dick arrived in Minneapolis only a short time before I did, but he brought with him about seventeen years of FAA experience, of which the last fourteen had been spent in various posts around Alaska. He may never before have been exposed to the big time, but nobody in Minneapolis was going to bring it to his attention.

One particular day, even a corporate pilot from Canada learned that Animal meant business when he spoke. We were working in the tower and Dick was working local control. He was responsible for all the traffic on the runways and also for all the traffic moving back and forth across them. Even though the ground controller was the person who actually talked to the pilots as they crossed, he first had to get approval from Dick, and therein was the problem. If Dick was too busy talking to his band of pilots as they arrived and departed from any one of three runways, the ground controller could do nothing with the other traffic as it waited to cross one of those active runways.

That created a couple of additional problems. One, it forced the ground controller to stop airplanes from crossing even if there was no doubt that the runway was clear of any conflicting traffic. Two, it also forced the ground controller to keep bugging the local controller for approval at a time when local least needed another distraction thrown his way. Either way, the result was that one or the other was driven a little crazier than usual.

Controllers, by nature or by habit, loathe having an airplane sitting still when their judgment tells them it's okay to move it. One reason is that experience has shown that airplanes going nowhere, whether sitting on the ground or holding in the air, only create the potential for getting in the way of other airplanes. The result is the attitude that when you can get them moving, do it! Then worry about the regulations later.

The other problem is that every controller knows what it's like to be busy, really busy. When one sees another in one of those situations, the last thing he wants to do is add more responsibility to the person who is "going down the pipe." Yet that's exactly what needed to be done. Because of several recent events around the country in which airplanes crossing runways almost became hood ornaments for other airplanes landing or taking off, the FAA had begun rigidly enforcing the rule that local control and only local control could give the authorization for such an action. Runway incursions, as they were called, were to become things of the past.

No longer could the ground controller use individual

judgment and direct traffic across the runway when it was safe to do so. That added responsibility was shifted to the local controller. In one sense that may be were it belonged all along, but in another it was throwing one more burden on a person who could already have been overloaded.

At busy airports, local controllers may be responsible for all the traffic on three or four different runways. When traffic heavy they are constantly looking six different ways, launching departures between arriving flights; making sure one plane doesn't cross another's runway until it is safe and legal; writing necessary information on flight progress strips; talking with the controllers in the radar room about various turns, speeds, and climbs; watching the radarscope to ensure adequate spacing exists on the final approach course; and yes, telling ground control it's okay to cross one of the runways. And all of this was supposed to be done at just about the same time.

While we may have liked to think of ourselves super-humans accomplishing the impossible, in truth it couldn't e done. Most of the time the regulation was circumvented by the round controller's emphatically stating something like, "Two nine left is clear. I'm crossing with one to the ramp!" At which point the cal controller would nod, wave a hand, or give some other indication that the message had been received. If worse came to worst, if there were four or five attempts and local still gave no indication that crossing the runway was approved, ground would simply yell, "I'm crossing NOW!" We figured the lack of denial somehow implied consent. If we didn't adhere to the letter of the law, certainly we paid tribute to its intent. The whole procedure may have been an exercise in futility anyway, because ten years later near misses on the runway are still all too common.

In a strange way, what occasionally compounded the problem of one controller talking to another was their headsets. The Plantronics Starset is a wonder of technological advancement, almost to a fault. Weighing no more than several ounces, the Starset can be comfortably hung on a controller's ear for hours without the slightest discomfort. The microphone portion of it, the boom, is an equally lightweight, tiny L-shaped piece of space-age material that, placed anywhere within twelve inches of the speaker's mouth, is capable of transmitting the meekest of voices hundreds of miles into space. The problem is that it can, and all too often does, send out conversations that are not meant for the ears of the flying public. When it does happen, at the very least someone on the frequency lets it be known that the controller's slip of the tongue was shared with everyone listening. At the worst, a phone call to the supervisor in the tower ensures that the blunder on the air is traced back to the person responsible.

Dick was in the midst of one of those happenings, the kind that almost every controller can relate to. He was right in the middle of a session of "pumpin' heavy tin," moving as many airplanes into and out of Minneapolis as the law would allow, and every now and then one or two more. He was having the kind of fun that keeps controllers coming back for more each day, but he was also extremely busy. Between the talking, looking, listening, pointing, and sending flight strips down the gravity tube to the radar controllers below, he had time for nothing else. Unfortunately, the King Air that had just arrived from Canada was sitting at the edge of the runway, eagerly waiting to cross.

At first he waited patiently. After a few minutes, when it became apparent that several opportunities to cross had come and gone without ground control's taking advantage of them, the pilot politely began prodding the controller. "Ah, Ground, you didn't forget about us waiting to cross did you?" Followed by, "We see the traffic on final and we can beat him across with no trouble." Each time his voice became less patient and more irritated.

In between each conversation with the pilot in the King Air, the ground controller moved closer and closer to Dick. With each step he took he spoke louder and louder. "Animal, the runway's clear, can I cross my King Air?" If Dick heard him, which in all likelihood he didn't, he was still too busy to answer. The ground controller decided to make one final attempt before initiating a slight regulation change. Only this time he leaned so close to Dick that there was no doubt that someone's personal space had been violated. As they stood there headset to headset in their little corner of the tower, ground yelled into Dick's ear, "If you hear me, nod your damn head. I'm crossin' two nine left!"

At that precise moment, still standing within a whisker's length of Dick, the ground controller keyed his microphone in anticipation of the nod that would legally allow the long-awaited crossing to occur. Also at that same exact moment, Dick decided to make it unquestionably clear that one, he didn't like having his space violated no matter what the reason, and two, if it wasn't the time to ask it was most assuredly the time to cross. With ground's mike still wide open, Dick yelled in a voice loud enough for half of Minnesota to hear, "Cross the fuckin' runway, and do it NOW!"

The King Air pilot had also heard the instructions. Whether he was so tired of waiting that the manner in which he received his clearance just didn't matter, or whether he became acutely aware that all those stories about the obnoxious Americans to the south were actually true, we didn't know. We witnessed, though, what had to be the fastest crossing of a runway by a turboprop aircraft since the beginning of federally assisted guidance. When the uncontrollable laughter in the tower finally subsided, no one felt worse about the misunderstanding than Dick.

There was no doubt that Dick had that special something that made controllers successful in the big time. For the first time since I started my career in the FAA, I wasn't so sure I could say the same of myself. Controlling airplanes had always come easily to me—at least that had been the case in Toledo. With the support of the rest of the crew and Al, training had been fun. They made me believe I could do the job, and I, in turn, believed in myself. Without too many exceptions, the attitude in Minneapolis was, we don't think you have what it takes and it's up to you to prove us wrong.

Part of the reason may have been that the battle lines were already being drawn for a strike that was still three years away. But with or without those tensions, Minneapolis Tower seemed to foster the existence of a different breed of controller, one that I hadn't seen before and, having met, one that I wasn't sure I ever wanted to see again. There was Marty, an ex–O'Hare controller and ex-supervisor. The best description of Marty came from the chief flight instructor for Thunderbird Aviation at Flying Cloud Airport. Marty and I both had reason to frequent Thunderbird—Marty because they had agreed to administer to the tower's flying club, of which he was president, and I because I was working on my various flight instructor ratings. As we sat there one day watching Marty expound upon one thing or another, the instructor looked at me and said, "The only way to think of Marty is as an island floating in a sea of ego." To me that seemed to say all there was.

Backing up Marty was Dale, another ex-supervisor who was

going to set the FAA straight. Dale came into his own one day in the radar room when he went head to head with a member of the evaluations team from our regional headquarters in Chicago. Once a year a team of specialists, most of whom hadn't worked traffic in years, traveled to each facility to see if everything was being run according to Hoyle or whoever else happened to be administrator at the time. To most of us it seemed like another exercise in futility, but we played along in the interest of job stability. If national headquarters was kept happy by regional headquarters, and regional headquarters was kept happy by the chiefs of the various facilities in the field, and the chiefs were kept happy by controllers playing along during evaluations week, then we were left alone for another year.

Dale apparently thought life was getting too boring at Minneapolis because he started needling the specialist sitting beside him. Exactly what was being said no one could say for sure. The two of them were far enough away from everyone else in the radar room that all we could hear was mumbling back and forth. Then Dale said whatever it was that made the regional representative decide enough was enough, at which point he shot up out of his chair, sent it sailing across the radar room, and stormed out yelling and swearing that Dale was one of the most disrespectful, obnoxious people he had ever met and our tower chief was going to hear about this. As the man made his exit, Dale just started to laugh.

Then came Gerry, unhappy about everything. Gerry was one of the few controllers I knew who chewed out a pilot because of a mistake he, not the pilot, had made. It happened as two North Central DC-9s were taxiing to runway 22. They first had to cross 29R, but they had to do it in between arrivals. The problem arose when Gerry mixed up the callsigns of the two airplanes. One had already crossed 29R safely. The other was just in the process of crossing when Gerry decided the arrival might arrive before the DC-9 was across the runway. So he issued instructions for the pilot to stop his aircraft, which the pilot on the other side of the runway promptly did. The second one, however, kept moving. Gerry yelled a second and then a third time before he realized what the problem was.

By then it was too late. The second DC-9 was far enough onto the runway that the arriving jet had to be issued a go-around.

No pilot likes to be told at the last minute to cancel the landing clearance, and airline pilots like it even less. It costs time and money. The end result was that everybody was unhappy, especially Gerry.

Whether or not it was true—and I secretly suspected it was—Gerry thought the pilots had made him look bad on purpose. Angrier than ever, he yelled into his mike, "That's okay, buddy, you have a good laugh over this cause your turn's comin' and that's a promise!" Gerry was one of those people who thought controlling would be a great job if it just wasn't for those damn airplanes.

Rounding out the crew were Bob, not as blatantly militant as the rest but still able to get his shots in whenever the mood struck; Dick, a master at the art of sarcasm; and Tom, the real brains and impetus behind the rest of the group. Individually, each was as kind and considerate a person as could be found anywhere. Collectively, they were responsible for much of the unrest that seemed to permeate the lives of everyone at Minneapolis Tower, and most particularly mine. They were also my crew, the men who would shape my future as an air traffic controller in the big time.

Charged with keeping them in line was a quiet, rather passive man named Jon, our supervisor. A longtime resident of Minneapolis Tower, Jon had been a controller, then a data systems specialist in charge of Tower computer operations, and finally a supervisor of the revolutionaries, a promotion that he later confided was not without regrets. An excellent controller and a kind, decent man, Jon was pleasant to be around. I liked Jon as a person, but as boss of the mean team, he was out of his league.

Although a few incredibly good supervisors occasionally slipped through the cracks of the screening process, most promotions in the FAA seemed based upon factors other than an individual's aptitude and ability to effectively manage people. Jon was not one of the exceptions. Only his concern for his family and his intense interest in cars kept him in his present position. Were it not for them, his career as a supervisor would have been very short-lived. Unfortunately, Jon's complete lack of authority meant that what happened between the rest of the crew and me was none of his business. I was on my own, and it wasn't a very comfortable place to be.

Fortunately, divine intervention seemed to come to my rescue in the strange and unexpected form of Tom. The same Tom who was the strategist for many of the union activities was also appointed to be my primary trainer, or "angel" as the FAA sometimes referred to the role. If ever there was a living, breathing paradox, Tom was it. Tall and thin, with a long, angular face accentuated by a beard and a mustache on the bottom and a full head of flesh on the top, he could have been easily mistaken for Paul Stookey of Peter, Paul, and Mary, except that Peter and Mary were never at his side.

But protest and confrontation were as much a part of Tom's nature as his appearance was a throwback to the unsettled days of the sixties. If he had missed out on the civil rights demonstrations and the Vietnam protests, which I'm not sure he did, then he made up for it by being a principal in the changes that were to take place within the FAA. A large part of the fire within Tom came from the fact that somehow, somewhere along the way, he became convinced that the FAA had severely taken advantage of his father. Tom's dad had retired from the FAA with less than father or son thought was deserved, and Tom was not about to give the Feds a chance to repeat that or a similar offense with him. With great vengeance and, I believe justification, Tom decided to become one of the watchdogs against abusive tactics within the FAA. Becoming active in PATCO on both the local and the national level was the best way to achieve that goal.

But Tom brought to Minneapolis other qualities besides his undying determination to push for change. Before becoming a controller, he had been a teacher. He continued to teach, not because the FAA said it was an integral part of every controller's job description but because he believed it was an essential part of his personal responsibility. To my surprise, as caustic and argumentative as Tom was with the supervisors and managers at the tower, he was patient and understanding with me. Instead of yelling insult upon insult, treatment often given to controllers in training, Tom carefully taught me much of what I needed to know to become a good controller at a major airport.

In spite of whatever claims the FAA may make about its advanced teaching and training techniques at the academy in Oklahoma City or anywhere else, almost all of a controller's real training comes in the form of on-the-job instruction. A rookie sits down in front of a radarscope filled with live traffic or stands in the tower looking directly at the opposition, plugs in the headset, and starts learning. Good instructors produce good controllers; bad instructors produce poor controllers. Some of the poor controllers improve significantly in spite of their initial training. Others remain exactly what they were the day their training ended—scared people hoping the odds never worked against them.

Much of my success as a controller, then, stems directly from the fact that Tom was my primary instructor. In ways that he probably never suspected, Tom really was my angel. I, in turn, was his shadow. Day after day, whenever he went to the tower to work, so did I. Whenever he went to the radar room, so did I. Whenever he was supposed to work in the radar room, an assignment preferred by most controllers, but traffic in the tower was such that training would be beneficial for me, Tom willingly gave up his time in radar and took me to the tower to train. When there was no useful training to be had in either the tower or the radar room, Tom would take me into the ETG (Enhanced Target Generator) room, and using the FAA's traffic simulator, he would teach me traffic procedures using computer-generated images of airplanes.

Tom was my primary instructor, but not my only instructor. One by one, the rest of my crew had the opportunity to teach me what they knew about air traffic control and what they didn't know about the milk of human kindness. Each had received the FAA's comprehensive eight-hour course in on-the-job training techniques and had been awarded the right to teach others the fine art of air traffic control. In reality, the selection process for instructors wasn't very selective and the training wasn't very comprehensive. If you were classified as a journeyman and you could breathe, you could teach. If you hadn't learned what you needed to know about teaching in the eight-hour program, it wasn't worth knowing. The result for me, and for a lot of others before and since my time, was that my life instantly became miserable enough to make me seriously consider giving up my career at Minneapolis.

After one too many grueling sessions with these malevolent despots, I went to our tower chief, Les, and told him enough was enough. I wanted out and I wanted out now. The big time wasn't any fun at all. The constant barrage of insults, temper tantrums, and sarcastic criticism, none of which seemed constructive to me, was more than I cared to live with. It was time to go home, and Toledo was home.

The events that followed my meeting with Les would

eventually have an impact on me that I couldn't foresee. Nor did I expect the immediate consequence of our conference. After about two hours of my giving him dozens of reasons why I should terminate my training and not one why I should stay, Les convinced me to stay anyway. Even more surprising was the crew's response.

Inside the FAA, the letters *RCC* have two completely different meanings, depending upon who is using them. Officially they stand for Rescue Coordination Center, the central point at which information regarding a lost airplane is collected and then disseminated to the search and rescue teams. Unofficially RCC stands for Rumor Control Center. The person or persons responsible for ensuring that anything of significance within a particular air traffic facility is quickly, not so quietly, and very efficiently passed on to every controller listed on the roles.

Within minutes of my leaving Les's office, word of my dissatisfaction started to spread among the troops. In less than an hour, everyone on duty that afternoon knew I wanted out of Minneapolis. Just as quickly, I started to feel more alone and vulnerable than I had ever felt in my life. I had exposed a weakness, and I knew it was just a matter of time before my bloodthirsty crew moved in for the kill. Regardless, I had promised Les that I would stay for at least another month or two. If my feelings hadn't changed by them, he would try to get me reassigned to Toledo. In the meantime I had to make the best of the situation I had created.

As I had suspected, my team members started to react to the news almost immediately. Tom was the first to approach me, and he caught me completely off guard with what he had to say. He told me that he thought leaving Minneapolis would be a very big mistake for me. He thought I had the talent and the ability to be one of their better controllers. Even more important to me, Tom said that he valued my friendship and on a personal level would be sorry to see me leave. Up to that point I had no idea that anyone, including Tom, thought of me as anything more than a liability with which my team was collectively stuck.

For the next thirty minutes or so, Tom went on to tell me that none of my emotions was unusual. Having come to Minneapolis from Rochester, Minnesota, an airport similar to Toledo, he knew everything I was going through because he had gone through the very same thing not too long before. Even if I didn't always like it, and I was sure that I wouldn't, I would learn to accept the ways and attitudes of the controllers there. He said that when I really got to know our crew I would realize they were basically good people.

I accepted most of what Tom said, but his last comment about the good guys seemed to be stretching things just a bit too far. When we were finished with our conversation, Tom asked me to wait in the ETG room for a minute. First came Dale and then Dick. Each echoed much of what Tom had said, but each also added a little bit more of themselves to the conversations. For the first time ever, I caught brief glimpses of their human sides.

Finally Jon, our supervisor, came in to talk with me. It was the first time since my arrival at Minneapolis that he and I ever had a conversation of any substance, but it was almost worth the wait. Although we said a lot of things to each other, I remember telling him that I could tell what day of the week it was by how big the knot was in my stomach. If it was the size of a basketball, I knew the next day would be my first day back to work. If it was almost nonexistent, I knew my weekend was about to start. Somewhere in between, and midweek was at hand.

What made it worse was that not only could I keep track of the days of the week by my emotional outlook, so could my family. The less pleasant I became, the closer it was to the beginning of my next round of shifts. Jon's answer to all of what I was telling him caught us both by surprise.

"If I didn't know better, I'd think you were describing my household. At least, that's what my wife would say."

If I was still feeling vulnerable, by the end of the evening I didn't feel quite as alone in my new job. Tom and the others all had taken a chance and shared a little of their weaknesses in a world that judges how good you are by how tough you can pretend to be. I knew it hadn't been easy for them, and that evening helped me get through a lot of the rough days that lay ahead.

Throughout the remainder of my training days at Minneapolis, not a whole lot changed. Tom was mostly still patient, but the rest of the crew continued much as they had before that evening. There were no more heart-to-heart talks, and my many mistakes were still a source of entertainment for any and all who were around when they occurred. I was the one who began to change.

I started to realize a couple of different things. When I had to, I could be authoritative enough to get pilots to listen to what I had to say. With the help of a few other controllers, who became my second crew, I also learned that I could do it without turning into a tyrant. Always waiting in the wings was Dick, showing me how to control traffic and still have fun, even if it occasionally meant turning into an animal. There were also Brad and another Tom, both ex–O'Hare controllers, who taught me that heavy traffic didn't always have to be handled with a heavy hand. From them I gained a perspective that would provide me with priceless insight many times in the future.

Mostly I learned that to be successful as an air traffic controller I had to have self-confidence far beyond that which I brought with me to Minneapolis. In a strange way I realized that I had my rowdy, belligerent first crew to thank for bringing that confidence to the surface. They taught me I could stand alone and be the controller I wanted to be. My second crew taught me that I could do it and still be the person I wanted to be. If ever the professional and personal aspects of my life couldn't coexist peacefully, it might be time for me to start looking for a different line of work.

BATTLE PLANS

I REMEMBER THE TELEVISION NEWS COVERAGE IN VIVID DETAIL. **The long-haired, bearded participants walked around in cutoff blue jeans and T-shirts, each waving one fist high in the air in a gesture of militant defiance against the government they felt had let them down. Yet it wasn't in protest of our country's involvement in a war on the other side of the world and it wasn't in support of any principle of racial equality. It was a strike by air traffic controllers, organized and led by PATCO, the Professional Air Traffic Controllers Organization.**

More than eight years later, I still have an abundance of mixed feelings about the whole situation. There are so many unanswered questions and unresolved issues that it seems the entire debacle occurred for no apparent reason. All that can be said for certain is that more than ten thousand usually law-abiding and responsible citizens defied their government and as a result permanently lost their jobs, jobs that most of them enjoyed most of the time. Whether or not the controllers were justified in their actions, it soon became obvious that when rational people start acting irrationally, regardless of which side of the bargaining table they are sitting on (and I believe they were on both), almost everyone loses.

The first day of the controllers' strike was August 3, 1981, but both sides began their battle plans long before the actual event took place. Decisions made more than three years earlier started the momentum that, once begun, was beyond any individual's power to stop, yet no one involved can be free of responsibility and blame for the results.

Since managers and supervisors had, in the past, always reaped the same or greater benefits from labor actions taken by controllers, many outwardly opposed but quietly supported the upcoming strike. Since controllers had always succeeded in winning major concessions whenever a sick-out or a slowdown was used to draw attention to their plight, they were completely convinced that past history would repeat itself. Since union members were becoming more and more dissatisfied with supporting the salaries of their national leaders when no changes in the substance or structure of their jobs seemed forthcoming, they put increased pressure on PATCO's leaders to produce. When mob psychology started to take over the day-to-day decision-making process, life became ugly for everyone involved.

Starting from the top, no one was immune. Due in large part to John Leyden, one of the original founders and the only president of PATCO, life for air traffic controllers had improved greatly since the sick-out of 1970. No longer were controllers required to spend four or five hours working a control position without a break. Nor did they have to eat their meals while simultaneously talking to pilots. If a controller believed that policies of the agency or actions of its representatives were detrimental to the public's safety or an individual's welfare, for the first time, official procedures existed to address the problems. PATCO and John Leyden were very much responsible for those changes. In spite of the fact that Leyden had gained a good deal of respect from most of the union members and many government officials in Washington, a select minority within PATCO began to ask, "But what have you done for us lately?"

The question was enough to instigate a power struggle in PATCO's national offices. When it was all over, John Leyden was out completely and Bob Poli was the new president of the union. Quickly, the entire character of the union started to change. Before the change in leadership, PATCO had received almost all of its direction from the membership at large. Issues were raised, sent to the controllers for comment and vote, and then resolved according to the majority opinion. Under Poli, the union, through its local and national officers, suddenly began telling its members what was, supposedly, best for them. The idea that each individual's opinion created a diversity of views that were valuable to the organization as a whole seemed to have become a thing of the past. In many ways the course that would lead to the August 3 strike had already been set.

The year 1978 witnessed the changes that would create a mood of discontent among controllers, even in places like Toledo. In the past, smaller air traffic facilities around the country had always been brought into PATCO's strategy almost as an afterthought. This time it was to be different. The union realized that, to be successful, it needed to have two things happen. First, it needed at least 95 percent of the active controllers to belong to PATCO. Second, it needed to have every one of those 95 percent participate in the planned strike. With that many controllers off the job, it seemed very unlikely that the FAA could safely maintain the air traffic system without major disruptions for air travelers. Without them, it seemed just as likely that the strike would fail and anyone who was involved with it would either be fired or jailed. The problem—how to make it all happen.

By nature, air traffic controllers tend to be strongly individualistic and highly opinionated. If two of them are put together in a room to resolve a problem, within an hour three factions will emerge, one for each opposing view of the problem and a third just in case the other two might result in an unintended compromise. The answer had to be to develop a common cause, something that would rally and bond all those different ideas and opinions into the brotherhood and sisterhood of PATCO. The problem still remained, how?

At the medium-sized airports like Toledo, organizing the controllers was actually harder than it was at the major airports. Life wasn't really that bad in the minor leagues. Occasionally we would get busy, even really busy. Because of the lack of modern equipment, when controllers got busy at Toledo, in some ways they worked harder than controllers at O'Hare or Atlanta ever worked. But they seldom did it for any great length of time, so when they weren't talking to a lot of pilots, stress and overwork weren't very high on the list of complaints.

Even pay didn't seem to be that much of a problem. For working forty hours a week, controllers in Toledo received a yearly salary in the high twenties or low thirties. Considering the relatively low cost of living in the area, the pay wasn't great but it seemed more than enough—until we started looking at other salaries. Did we realize that airline pilots receive two or three times as much money for working about half the time we did? Did we know that bus drivers in San Francisco made as much as controllers? Even a senior flight attendant made as much as a controller for working about as much as the pilots did. How would we like a $10,000 across-the-board increase?

The almost unanimous answer, "Yeah! Let's go for it! What do we have to do?"

Having gotten our attention with thoughts of a well-deserved pay raise, PATCO went on to address some of the real issues that bothered controllers everywhere, including Toledo. Supervision, or lack of it, was one of the more important ones. Whether it was indirect supervision in the form of an archaic policy handed down from someone in an obscure office in Washington who hadn't even seen a radarscope since jets were invented, or the more direct supervision in the radar room, there did seem to be room for improvement.

Controllers have had and still have a very low opinion of FAA management talent. The saying has long been, "If a controller has enough near misses he'll be made a supervisor; if he has a midair collision he gets to be a manager." Although maybe a little too harsh, and certainly not universally true, the saying unfortunately carries with it some truth.

Supervisors are most often promoted directly from the ranks of controllers. If they have any natural ability, after four weeks of training at the FAA management school, they begin their careers as supervisors. If they have neither ability nor desire, after four weeks of training at the FAA management school, they still begin their careers as supervisors. Either way they start making daily decisions that affect how easily or how well controllers can do their jobs.

At one point the problem of poor decisions became so prevalent that PATCO negotiated into the controllers' contract a provision known as Article 55. Simply stated, Article 55 said that if a supervisor ordered a controller to make a control decision that, in the controller's opinion, would have an adverse effect on safety, the supervisor would accept all responsibility for the consequences of the action. Unfortunately for everyone involved, Article 55 had more than its fair share of use. A bad decision is a bad decision, regardless of who bears the responsibility for it. The good news was that the threat of invoking Article 55 was more than enough to cancel a supervisor's order. Either way, unnecessary stress and abundant ill will were created.

Some of the worst problems occurred outside the realm of air traffic control. One of the most frustrating examples involved Pat, someone I knew as a likable and cooperative controller. Prior to an afternoon shift, Pat found his future as a controller seriously in jeopardy when a sudden gust of wind blew powdered chlorine that was meant for his swimming pool into one of his eyes.

An emergency trip to his doctor left Pat with a large patch over one eye and the uncertainty of having to wait a few days to find out if any permanent damage had occurred. For obvious reasons, controllers need two good eyes to safely perform their job. For the same obvious reasons, someone used to driving with two good eyes shouldn't suddenly attempt to drive with one eye covered. If those weren't cause enough for Pat to stay home from work that day, there was the added danger that legitimate worries about his family's future welfare might interfere with the intense concentration required by his job.

Yet when he called the tower to request sick leave, his request was denied. The supervisor on duty advised him that if he didn't report for duty at the appointed hour, he would be considered AWOL (absent without leave) and would be docked a day's pay. Pat went to work, but one by one, each of his crew said we would begin the shift only after declaring it was being worked under Article 55. Not so slowly the light dawned, and Pat was sent back home. It would be almost ten years and ten thousand controllers later before I personally learned that managers with such a complete lack of human understanding still existed within the FAA.

Little by little we started thinking that maybe our jobs weren't so great after all. What about training? Every controller was required to provide on-the-job training for new controllers. Since facilities like Toledo were the proving ground for almost every developmental controller who came out of the FAA Academy in

Oklahoma City, daily training sessions were and still are very much the norm. To meet the demand, every journeyman controller in the country was given the intense eight-hour course in OJT (on-the-job) instruction and, upon graduation, duly dubbed an instructor.

Controllers who had had worthwhile, valuable experiences when they were in training usually went on to become highly productive teachers. Controllers who had been subjected to various forms of abuse, insult, and neglect during the course of their learning process just as frequently passed that treatment along to the next unsuspecting victim. Regardless, being the provider of OJT instruction was often a thankless task that required twice the effort of working alone and resulted in little more than an occasional pat on the back and orders to get back in there an do it again.

Meanwhile, we were continually reminded that if 95 percent of us would stick together and strike, it would take years to train enough new controllers to replace us. The FAA would have to give in to our demands. Brothers and sisters, we can do it!

There were other issues too. In an organization the size of the federal government, employee benefits seemed to pale when compared to private industry. In an era of high inflation, government employees were repeatedly asked to set the standard by being content with annual salary increases of 2 or 3 percent, even when the rest of the country was less than eager to follow their lead. And most important, what about all those things PATCO had already done for us? Didn't the union deserve our unswerving allegiance in the troubled times that surely lay ahead? Remember, it's us against them now.

The rhetoric had an effect even in Toledo, where in the past the thirty or so controllers, supervisors, and managers had often worked, played, and lived together like a family in spite of opposing views. Life began to change noticeably for those few controllers who had chosen, for whatever personal reasons, not to belong to PATCO. Some controllers had always harbored a certain resentment against nonunion controllers, who received all the benefits of union representation without having to pay any dues, and that resentment started to become more openly displayed.

It had always been common practice for the controllers just coming on duty to relieve the previous shift's controllers ten or fifteen minutes early so they could go home on time. The new practice for some became to do this only for the union controllers. If the person waiting to go was nonunion, let him wait until the last minute. The more pressure applied now, the greater the chances that the holdout would join the union. The more who joined the union, the more who would strike when the time came, and of course the greater the odds for success.

At the same time, the rift between controllers and management continued to grow. Facility parties and picnics during which everyone forgot about rank became fewer and fewer. Word came down from above that a supervisor who stopped at the local pub for a drink with his crew after work probably wasn't putting the best interest of the FAA first. When the time came for that supervisor to receive additional consideration of any kind, that fact would just as probably not be forgotten. In general, friends who had talked freely and openly and who had agreed that there was common cause for all to be concerned soon started becoming selective and secretive in their choices of confidants and subjects.

For me it seemed the time was right to move on to another airport. Toledo Express Airport had been very good for me. I learned there many of the basic skills that would help me throughout the rest of my career as a controller. I gained the beginnings of the confidence that would help me allay the doubts and fears that were to surface in the future. And I learned how it felt to be a member of a team, to rely upon other people and to have them rely upon me.

Most of all, I had found a lot of friends, a few of whom turned out to be among my very best. Each had given a part of themselves to me, and I wanted to leave before the events that were happening could take it back. I sent out bids to several different airports in the Great Lakes region, and I was happy to accept a position in Minneapolis when it was offered to me in November 1978.

Rumor had it that Minneapolis was a nice place to live and that the tower was an equally pleasant place in which to continue my career. A visit earlier in the year seemed to confirm the rumors. All that was left was to say good-bye to everyone and everything that Toledo had been to me.

As I said my farewells, I had no idea that all our lives would change so drastically so soon. Ron would stick it out as a controller, get divorced, and marry another controller who also crossed the picket lines. Almost all the remaining controllers I knew lost their jobs and went their separate ways.

Although I've driven past Toledo airport several different times since we left, I couldn't bring myself to go in and visit. Most of the controllers there would be strangers to me. If there were any I knew, I strongly suspected that the common friendship we once had would seem as though it had never really been there at all. No matter which side of the strike we had stood on, each of us had changed too much to forget.

THE GAP WIDENS

IF THE TROOPS WERE STARTING TO GET RESTLESS WHEN I LEFT TOLEDO, by the time I arrived in Minneapolis a week or so later the battle was already raging. The gap between controllers and management had widened to a chasm with both sides acting more irrational and unprofessional as each day went by.

What clouded the whole issue was that neither side was completely right or wrong. Moreover, both sides had such a complex array of characters—all of whom could alter their personas at a moment's notice—that from day to day I was never really sure where I stood with respect to the planned strike.

At the heart of the FAA's argument was the fact that each and every controller, prior to being employed by the federal government, had signed a written oath stating they would take no job action against their employer. To do otherwise was simply illegal, and although controllers are individualistic by nature, they are also basically moderate and conservative by politics. With few exceptions, the majority of controllers wanted little or nothing to do with the idea of a strike. Through a strange twist of irony, that attitude may have had a lot to do with the fact that just the opposite occurred.

As events moved closer and closer to the final confrontation, our daily activities became more and more absurd. PATCO started to intensify its attacks on the FAA and the nonunion controllers who hadn't yet seen the light. One of the plans was to bury the FAA under paperwork by filing union grievances for anything and everything. If the FAA was kept busy enough responding to these grievances, there would be little time left for them to counter the effects of the strike when it occurred. At one point our local union filed a grievance against the management because the facility secretary had been found hanging her coat on the controllers' coatrack.

Attention was then turned to the scabs, those holdouts who just wouldn't join PATCO. In addition to the now-routine practice of providing them with less than timely relief from the control positions, social shunning and an even more serious practice with equally serious safety implications started to develop. Nonunion controllers working live traffic were not given the support they needed from fellow controllers. In a few rare instances, errors unknowingly made by nonunion controllers were allowed to continue with the hope that a breach in safety would convince them how much they needed their fellow union controllers.

The most blatant example of this practice was offered by none other than our local PATCO president. A recent change in one of our letters of agreement, a written procedural statement between two air traffic facilities, helped to create the problem. In the old letter, traffic we sent northbound on a particular airway was to be at four thousand feet. Traffic coming into our airspace on that same airway was to be assigned three thousand feet. Although changes could and often were made on an individual basis with coordination between the controllers working each airplane, as a rule the letter provided pilots with a built-in safety margin of one thousand feet of separation. If either pilots or controllers lost their ability to communicate with one another, there was no danger of a midair collision.

As the FAA is all too frequently wont to do, in the new letter of agreement it reversed the past procedure. Under the new letter our traffic would depart our airspace at three thousand feet and arrive inbound at four thousand feet. Anything else would have to be approved ahead of time.

Controllers are creatures of habit, even more so than the average person. From the very first day of training they are instructed to develop patterns for as many of their tasks as is humanly possible. A large percentage of airport traffic is handled in exactly the same manner, so if a certain procedure becomes almost automatic for controllers, then what they do most likely will be correct, even if their level of concentration is not 100 percent. More important, if most of their actions don't require a lengthy thought process for correct instructions to be issued to pilots, then when an unusual or emergency situation does develop, their extra time can be spent resolving the unexpected problem. In the case of a new procedure, several weeks of careful attention are required before the old habits are replaced with the new.

One morning a nonunion controller who was working the north satellite position reverted to the old practice and sent a pilot northbound on the airway at four thousand feet. Without coordination with the receiving controller responsible for the next segment of airspace, a system deviation would occur as soon as the airplane crossed our airspace boundary. The controller responsible for the occurrence would be guilty of violating air traffic regulations and would be dealt with accordingly. If during the deviation the airplane was allowed to get closer to another airplane than is permitted by those same regulations, a system error would result. Most of the time a deviation is prevented from turning into an error only by sheer luck.

Usually if a controller makes a mistake that he or she doesn't catch right away, someone else in the radar room or tower will notice it before a problem arises. Such situations are part of the planned redundancy of the system, and most often they work just the way they were intended. This situation could have and should have been concluded with equal ease, except that a few people had other ideas.

One of them, our president, saw the problem developing. Rather than telling the controller of the impending error, he quietly punched into the intercom line with the receiving controller and made other arrangements. He told the other controller of the violation in procedures that was about to occur and asked him to wait until the airplane had crossed the boundary. Then he should report the incident as a deviation. The receiving controller agreed.

Within minutes of the mistake, the controller in question was relieved of his duty and an investigation was initiated. He openly admitted to the transgression, and the tape recording of his conversations was pulled as evidence for the explanation of what had happened. Since a single tape records all the different control positions within the radar room, during the investigation the whole ugly plot came to the surface.

Two conclusions were drawn from the information. One was that during his conversation with the controller from the other facility, our union president had, in effect, taken care of the required coordination before the airplane left our airspace. Although his intentions were clearly to cause trouble, the necessary information about the plane being at the wrong altitude had been given to the receiving controller in time. There had been no system deviation.

The other more important conclusion was that, obviously, our president had acted in a manner that wasn't in accordance with either the letter or the spirit of air traffic procedures. He had intentionally allowed a potentially unsafe situation to continue when he had had the ability to prevent it. The punishment he received for his actions—a reprimand with the instructions never to do it again.

PATCO's activities became more unreasonable, and the core of union leaders became more militant. Those of us who considered ourselves moderate, believing that someone or something would intervene before a strike was allowed to develop, began divorcing ourselves from the association that was supposedly representing us. But by doing so, we and many others throughout the country took that moderation away from the union and left the organization solely in the hands of those people we thought were most militant. What happened as a result of our apathy was as much our fault as theirs, and a lot started to happen.

Every union meeting became nothing more than a soapbox for those who believed we had the power to cripple the nation and that if we didn't use that power to get what we wanted, we were fools. Anyone who spoke out against the proposed actions of the union was instantly chastised and silenced by the outraged cries of the leaders. Eventually many of us quit going to the meetings altogether.

One of the last meetings I attended before a sense of utter hopelessness finally overtook me had as its guest speaker an air traffic controller from Canada. PATCO had learned from past experience that not including controllers' spouses in the decision-making process was a serious mistake, and the union had vowed not to repeat the error. In attendance that night were controllers from Minneapolis Tower and Minneapolis Center and most, if not all, of their respective mates. We were there to hear why going out on strike was such a successful maneuver, at least for the controllers in Canada.

Over the course of the next hour or so, this controller told us how, as a result of the strike in Canada, controllers there now worked a thirty-two-hour week instead of our forty-hour week. For the time they did work and for the amount of traffic they handled, they were also making more money than controllers in the United States made. One of the last things the speaker said was, "I personally wish you folks would strike too. You see, when we were in negotiations we used to be able to say that our brothers and sisters to the south were making more than we were. But now we can't say that anymore."

Amid the laughter and the applause that swept the room after his comment, one last question and our speaker's very quiet answer went almost unnoticed. The question was, "Is it true that controllers in Canada legally have the right to strike against the government?"

His answer, simply, "Yes."

On the other side of the fence, while all this was happening, was FAA management. To many of us it seemed that if there was a collective philosophy or a common plan it was to give the union enough rope and it would hang itself. In retrospect it seems that the FAA and the federal government secretly did everything possible to ensure that a strike would develop.

Manager after manager and supervisor after supervisor complained of having little if any ability to intervene in almost any crisis for fear of incurring the wrath of the union. They saw themselves as helpless. One day a controller in Minneapolis was physically beating up another controller in the middle of the radar room, and no one stepped in to stop the fight.

As was so often the case, whether it was a matter of refereeing a fight or settling a dispute about traffic handling procedures, controllers were left to police themselves. Sometimes it worked, but most of the time it was about as effective as one ten-year-old keeping another from stuffing a hand in the cookie jar. The idea might have been good, but the power behind the enforcer was nonexistent. Everyone, including most of the controllers, wanted something done to restore order to the situation, but nobody knew exactly how to do it.

Even the team supervisors who in the past had been able to bridge the gap between labor and management tired of the daily battles. In Minneapolis alone, four supervisors had cut back their careers and their paychecks to return to the controller ranks. In a couple of the cases it was management's gain and our loss, but with one person in particular, everyone ended up losing.

Once in a long while, we all get to meet one of those people who just seems too good to be true. When I do, I secretly look long and hard to find at least some little flaw that will bring that paragon closer to my level of imperfection. With Bob I was never able to find that flaw. He turned out to be as good as he seemed that first day I met him at the airport.

Quiet and soft-spoken, always with a smile on his face, Bob brought to Minneapolis all those good qualities that one might guess would be the result of having been raised in the simple, honest, hardworking tradition of a Midwest dairy farm. It was difficult if not impossible to get him to say anything bad about anyone or anything. His primary job at the tower was as a computer systems specialist. On occasion, though, he worked traffic just because he still loved to do it, and no matter how badly I screwed up the traffic before it got to him, he always had time to boost my morale a little.

Through a strange quirk of fate that ended up making us neighbors, we also became good friends outside of work. Bob was as good a friend as he was a co-worker. Not long after my family and I moved to the great north country, he showed just how good that could be. My other neighbors, in what I thought was some sort of sick-minded initiation thrust upon a foreigner faced with his first Minnesota winter, had told me I needed to shovel the snow off the roof of my house before it caved it in. Bob did more than talk.

He knew I believed the whole thing was just a plot to provide the neighborhood with some cheap entertainment. But he also knew that if I didn't do something soon there was a very real danger that the roof would collapse under the weight of almost four feet of snow that had fallen since Thanksgiving. Bob went to work on his own, and by the time I arrived home from the tower he had already cleaned off more than half of a very large roof. In spite of the below-zero temperatures and the blustery northern winds that had been blowing all day, Bob met me with his usual big smile and wave when I pulled into the driveway, still in my toasty, warm car.

Whatever he did, Bob made sure that he accomplished the task with all the pride and ability he could possibly muster, so it was more than a pleasant surprise when he was selected to be our next supervisor at Minneapolis. The surprise came not because he had the desire and the ability to do the job but because the FAA had recognized it. It was one of those few instances in the FAA when everyone at the tower, save the people who were competing against him for the job, was pleased with the selection.

Controllers who had worked with Bob were confident that he knew what it took to control the traffic at Minneapolis effectively. They also knew he was capable of managing the people under his direction as fairly and as competently as possible. On the other side, his bosses also knew that, whatever the situation, Bob would handle it as well or better than any other supervisor there. For as long as the honeymoon lasted, everyone was happy that Bob was a supervisor at Minneapolis.

But the honeymoon didn't last very long. After a short while, Bob had to walk that thin line. If he followed through on a directive that came down from above, regardless of whether or not it had any merit in the world of air traffic, the union would be upset with him just on general principles. If he chose not to enforce the latest edict or to bend it into a more workable proposition, then the agency he was representing would be just as irritated. Bob found out first hand what a lot of other team supervisors had known all along. He had the one job in the facility for which, no matter what he did, he was bound to catch hell from both sides.

Under the best of conditions, being responsible for the conduct and general welfare of six, eight, or ten temperamental, occasionally egotistical, air traffic controllers can be cause for a certain amount of stress. With all the prestrike activities in full swing, the added stress on supervisors seemed even more formidable than that which we controllers were facing. And while all the controller-management hassles were escalating to ever-increasing levels, the daily chore of working a lot of airplanes into and out of

Minneapolis never eased up. The combination of the two left little time for any of us to find ways to reduce or relieve the building tension.

On this count Bob was no different from the rest of the cast at Minneapolis, but I didn't realize how much it was affecting him until one afternoon when he stopped by the house to talk. It seemed he had been giving a lot of serious thought to resigning his position as a supervisor and going back to being a controller. In spite of the years of hard work it had taken him to finally make it into the management ranks, he said that it just didn't seem worth it anymore. What he liked most about the job was talking to pilots and vectoring airplanes. Everything else that was going on had taken all the fun out of that.

When he needed the FAA to support his decisions, the backing was hardly ever there. When he needed the cooperation of the controllers to get a particular job done, it was nowhere to be found. As if I were hearing myself speaking through someone else, Bob said that after all his years in the FAA, he just didn't enjoy going to work anymore. He thought that if he went back to being a controller at least he would have the satisfaction of doing the job he had always loved.

After several months and countless, agonizing hours of deciding, Bob did resign as a supervisor at Minneapolis. For a while, at least, he seemed happier. The burden of trying to do the right thing for everyone without tools enough to do it for anyone was gone. In its place was a certain contentment that came from doing a job he knew and doing it as well as anyone could.

Bob was not the only one facing a burdensome decision. In October 1980, something compelled me to make a career decision that would later affect me in ways I couldn't begin to imagine at the time. Once again I felt it was time to say good-bye to the FAA for what I was absolutely sure was the very last time.

Several things seemed painfully obvious to me. The strike was definitely coming, and there didn't seem to be much that anyone could do to stop it. The momentum created by PATCO had been building for over a year, and with each passing day it seemed as though more and more controllers started to believe that we deserved a ten-thousand-dollar-a-year pay raise and that if we all stuck together we could actually get it. While we may not have been irreplaceable in the long term, almost everyone in the controller ranks resolutely believed we were indispensable in the short term. So did I.

In spite of the fact that the FAA had been stockpiling management and staff personnel for over a year, none of us thought for a minute that that hodgepodge collection of extras could step in and fill our shoes. With a few notable exceptions, it seemed that most of them had chosen a different career track precisely because they couldn't handle the day-to-day job of safely moving a lot of traffic. Now the government was expecting these same air traffic misfits to take over the entire system under uniquely difficult circumstances and maintain the "safe, orderly, and expeditious flow of traffic" for an indeterminate period of time. On that point I was as convinced as anyone. It just couldn't be done without seriously compromising safety.

If the FAA couldn't control its work force under the present conditions, it seemed obvious to a lot of us that it would be in a much worse position to do so after a successful strike. If brawling in the radar room and concern about who's hanging whose coat on which coatrack were legitimate or acceptable behaviors when the union hadn't even used its big guns, we wondered what would be the accepted norms after PATCO showed everyone who really was in charge. So far, no one in a position of authority had shown the slightest inclination to slow the rising tide of militancy exhibited by union leaders. Nor were there any indications that, if and when a strike took place, those controllers who remained faithful to their oaths would get much support from the government.

While it was true that threats of jail terms for PATCO leaders and mass firings for other strikers were commonplace around most ATC facilities, these were planned future actions. Nothing in the history of the FAA gave anyone good reason to believe those threats would become reality. On the other hand, the union's threats of physical violence and permanent career disruption for controllers who didn't participate in the strike seemed all too well founded. Past labor strife in this country often had been marred by violence. Why should a PATCO strike be any different?

But that's exactly what the FAA and the government were asking controllers to believe. If you go out on strike, either you will be fired or you will go to jail. Anyone who does strike will not be allowed to return to work, ever. If you choose to stay on the job, we, as representative of the United States government, will ensure safety for you and your family by whatever means necessary. This time we are not kidding.

The overwhelming response from controllers was, "Yeah, right."

While controllers everywhere were waging their own personal battles over what was the right thing to do, what was best for their families, and who had the best odds of coming out on top, my choice turned out to be the least of all the evils, as I saw them. Having already turned down a supervisor's job at Flying Cloud Airport because I just wasn't ready to give up controlling, my chosen lot in the FAA seemed clear. If I stayed in air traffic, at least for the immediate future, it would be as a controller. From that point on, the rest of my choices became a lot less obvious.

Would I or should I go on strike? Not so strangely, one of my first thoughts was of my father. Up until his death a few years earlier, he had also been my attorney of record since my birth. As such he instilled in me a strong regard for both the law and the government that was sworn to uphold it. As much as he suffered when first my brother and then I spent consecutive tours of duty in Vietnam, he believed in serving the country to protect those same laws for future generations. What would he have thought if I participated in an illegal strike?

A conservative Republican in his later years, my father had started his law career fighting for the rights of coal miners in Western Pennsylvania in the early thirties and forties. As incongruous as it might have seemed, he also taught me that if you believed in something strongly enough, it was your duty to use every means possible to support that belief, including fighting the system when everything else had failed. The question then for me became, did I believe that strongly in anything PATCO was doing, and if I did, was a strike the best or only possible means to make that belief a reality?

Despite my convoluted thought process, the truth was I did believe in some of the things PATCO was fighting for. I had received a pay raise with my promotion to Minneapolis, but inflation and a higher cost of living had eaten up almost all of it. Our family had had a higher standard of living in Toledo. If the FAA required controllers to move three or four times as they climbed the bureaucratic ladder, then we weren't being compensated enough for our efforts.

As for a four-day work week, that was one area in which I believed a comparison between pilots and controllers was appropriate and necessary. For reasons of stress, scheduling, and fatigue, airline pilots never worked a forty-hour week. Controllers too bore a certain amount of responsibility for the safety of passengers, and they worked as many as three different shifts within one week, yet frequently they were asked to put in an extra day of overtime. Eventually, the heavier traffic of the large airports took its toll on even the best controllers.

As much as I disagreed with many of PATCO's tactics, if I didn't go on strike I would essentially be supporting the FAA and its management policies, and that wasn't exactly where I wanted to be either. To a very great extent, I was where I was because of the controllers who had helped me get there. Time after time, other controllers went out of their way to help my family and me feel welcome in a new area. At sometimes great strain to themselves, other controllers taught me almost everything I needed to know to be a good controller. With more than just a remote risk of reprimand, other controllers covered for me when I made the inevitable learning mistakes of a new controller. In short, when the balance was weighed, it seemed as though I owed other controllers a lot more than I owed the rest of the FAA.

Finally though, the decision came down to what did I owe my family and—the more selfish consideration—what did I owe myself. Of two things I was certain. The strike by PATCO was coming, exactly when I didn't know, but it was too late for either side to turn back. When it came, the union would successfully shut down the nation's air traffic for two or three weeks. When the government realized it couldn't overcome the deficit of trained controllers, it would again cave in to most of PATCO's demands. Then those same union leaders who had led the strike and who were largely responsible for replacing reason and logic with unreasoned anger and bitterness would be running the whole show. Anyone who had walked with them would be safely entrenched in a PATCO–controlled FAA. Anyone who had been foolish enough to believe government claims of protection would be sitting in no-man's land, but most assuredly not for very long.

Whatever happened, the job of controlling air traffic and the atmosphere in which it would be accomplished was going to be decidedly different in the future. It was evident that the air traffic controllers in the poststrike FAA would approach their jobs with a completely different attitude than had been common in the past.

With no more than a passing thought about whether the FAA could miraculously hold the system together without most of its experienced controllers, I made my decision. It had been fun, a lot of fun. But now it was time to pack the family up, move back to Pennsylvania, and say good-bye to the FAA, if not forever, for a very long time. Whatever happened would be somebody else's problem. I would have enough of my own to keep me busy.

SHOCK AND AFTERSHOCK

FOR ME, LEAVING ANY OF MY DUTY STATIONS HAD ALWAYS BEEN a lot like saying good-bye to family. Leaving Minneapolis proved to be the same. Regardless of our personal differences, and even regardless of how we had stood on PATCO's activities, we could rely on each other when a traffic situation at work got tense. Just like a family, we felt it was okay to fight among ourselves, but when an outsider threatened to endanger our welfare, we put momentary disputes on hold until the danger had passed.

What made leaving Minneapolis even harder was the complete uncertainty with which I said my good-byes to everyone. We were all sure that a strike wasn't too far in the future, and my closest friends were just as sure that when the time came they would have no choice except to follow PATCO's lead. The circumstances under which we might meet in the future were anyone's guess.

It was with deep regret that I left my second crew. They were among the very best I had ever worked with and some of my very closest friends. As is so often true, we said we would continue to keep in touch with one another. Meant it. But somehow we knew that, even as we were saying it, it wasn't going to be true.

Instead I remember them through a gift they gave me that hangs on my office wall, wherever my office happens to be. It's a simple square of galvanized metal fastened to an old piece of Minnesota barnwood by a nail at each corner and intricately hand-engraved with the following: VAN BRENLOVE, A MAN FOR ALL REASONS . . . CONTROLLER PILOT TRAVELER SCRIVENER. Alongside each of the four "hats" I had worn at one time or another is an etching of a tool that matches the particular calling. At the bottom of the plaque in their own script are all the crewmembers' signatures. I could only hope the FAA would be smart enough not to lose them in the days ahead.

At my request, from Les, chief of the tower, I received a glowing letter of recommendation to be used whenever or wherever I chose. But for all its splendor, my final communiqué from the FAA had its own bitter irony. One sentence referring to articles I had written for a local aviation magazine called the *Minnesota Flyer* stated, "Portions of the articles were printed verbatim in other publications, including a letter to airmen by the local FAA General Aviation District Office to *all* Minnesota pilots." What the letter didn't say, but what Les knew, was that the portions used were plagiarized by the safety inspector who signed and issued the letter to airmen. A small infraction maybe, but the sight of my exact words above someone else's signature left the entire FAA none the dearer to my heart.

No less disappointing was my final gift from Minneapolis Tower, an official FAA plaque. Weighing about a pound and a half more than the barnwood plaque, my highly varnished imitation teakwood plaque bearing the official FAA seal, a beautifully engraved picture of the tower, and my name with the dates of service to Minneapolis lies stashed away in the back of my file cabinet. While more aesthetically pleasing to the eye than my crew's handmade gift, it was worth a lot less to me.

As sorrowful as the parting was, I knew I had made the right decision. In the days ahead I could only watch, wait, and hope the same would be true for those who were left behind.

During the late winter and early spring of 1981, nothing terribly new or surprising came out of either battle camp. Both PATCO and the FAA worked to solidify their respective plans and, in doing so, to capture the attention of the nation's air travelers. PATCO repeatedly said that the union now had the numbers it needed to successfully shut down the system, and the FAA just as frequently responded that it was ready to take over and keep the airlines flying. Meanwhile, most people close to the real situation would only guess how everything might turn out.

As a freelance writer and flight instructor, I struggled to survive in the small but serene town of Mercer, Pennsylvania. Located about sixty miles north of Pittsburgh, Mercer was the ideal place for a budding writer to commune with nature. It just wasn't the place to make a living. With still no conscious intention of ever returning to the FAA, I watched and listened for any news of the planned strike.

Occasional calls to and from Toledo and Minneapolis only served to confirm what I already knew or suspected: other than getting more and more heated, the situation hadn't changed. I did find out, however, that Pat had been selected for a data systems job in Toledo and, of all people, good old Dick, the Animal, had been made a supervisor in Minneapolis. I was exceedingly happy to hear about their promotions, not only because at least two friends would be spared any unpleasant consequences of the strike but also because two qualified, dedicated people had infiltrated the ranks of FAA management.

Then, in early summer with the first strike date hours away, the FAA offered PATCO a settlement package. Besides giving in to several less newsworthy items, in an unprecedented move, the FAA offered controllers what amounted to about a 5 percent increase in wages. With the approval of Congress, controllers would receive that increase above and beyond the normal civil service raises that affected all government employees.

It was the first time ever that PATCO had successfully made wages a part of its contract negotiations, and although the 5 percent offer was substantially less than what the union was seeking, the prospects for future pay negotiations seemed high. To the controllers I talked with, it seemed to be just the thing that could stop the momentum of a strike. All that was needed was for PATCO's national officers to sell the package to the membership and the worst would be over.

The initial relief many of my friends felt turned out to be short-lived. Disregarding what seemed to be obvious political and economical considerations, PATCO's leaders advised controllers to hold out for their original demands. If the FAA was willing to offer

5 percent, the government had to have seen the strength of the union's position. With a few more strong-arm tactics, a better offer had to be only days away. The offer was officially voted down, but pending the resumption of negotiations controllers agreed to delay their decision to strike.

What controllers and their representatives didn't pay attention to were events going on in Washington and the rest of the country. Although Ronald Reagan had voiced his concern for the plight of controllers prior to his election, in his relatively new role as president of the United States, he changed his approach. Bowing to the threat of an illegal strike against the government would do little to enhance his posture as a law-and-order president.

Adding to Reagan's pressure to stand firm against PATCO was the potential threat of the postal workers union. It was common knowledge around the country that the postal workers were anxiously awaiting the outcome of the controllers' negotiations. They were soon to begin their own round of talks, and what they did depended in large part upon how successfully PATCO negotiated its contract. If controllers went out on strike and won, the postal workers would most likely follow suit.

Public sentiment and support, or lack of it, were of critical importance. In the sluggish economy of 1981, new labor contracts had become synonymous with wage concessions and layoffs. It was all but impossible to arouse sympathy for controllers from the population at large, who shared the general feeling that, as a rule, all government employees are overpaid and underworked. Most controllers were already making more money than the people they were asking to support them. Even the labor unions that had promised to walk out in support of PATCO started backing out one by one. It soon became evident to almost everyone that if the controllers did eventually go on strike, they would be doing it alone.

Meanwhile, the day-to-day working conditions for controllers and supervisors alike just became worse. Anytime a dispute arose, controllers would say, "Wait until we get back after the strike." Supervisors would respond, "You won't be coming back this time. You'll be in jail." Beneath all the brazen comments, frustrations grew and tension mounted. Bob Poli, probably sensing that the controller's dissatisfaction was as much directed at himself and PATCO's national negotiating team as it was at the FAA, must have decided it was time to act. In what seemed more an effort to save his own job rather than concern for what controllers would gain, and despite all evidence to the contrary, Poli and the rest of PATCO's leaders called for the strike.

On August 3, 1981, most of the nation's air traffic controllers walked off their jobs. Within minutes air travelers everywhere were stranded. Within hours President Reagan went on national television and ordered controllers back to work, saying that anyone who didn't obey the order would be summarily fired. In Pittsburgh, USAir cancelled 90 percent of its flights and said that resumption of service would be on a graduated basis pending the success of the FAA's contingency plan. In Mercer, I watched with mixed emotions as I wondered how effective the strike would be.

The first few days brought no more than a trickle of controllers back to work, and while travel by air was being severely disrupted, most everyone seemed willing to hang on. PATCO urged its members to do the same as it repeatedly warned the public that anyone who flew was playing their own brand of Russian roulette. It was only a matter of time before the lack of qualified controllers brought about a serious air disaster.

With every controller, ex-controller, and many of the FAA's own managers convinced they could never pull it off, the FAA put its contingency plan into full operation. Supervisors, managers, staff personnel, tower chiefs, and anyone else in the FAA who had ever worked a day as a controller were put to work. Filling in the gaps wherever they could were hundreds of military controllers, trying desperately to adapt to the civilian way of doing business. Outside on the sidewalks were the PATCO controllers, their husbands and wives and children, still marching with fists held defiantly in the air.

As each new day dawned without the predicted airline crashes littering the countryside, information about the strike moved farther and farther toward the back of the news. Reagan stood firm on his position that the fired controllers would not be rehired under any circumstances, and pilots and passengers alike seemed to support his decision. Keeping in touch with friends in Toledo and Minneapolis, I found PATCO's position hadn't changed either. Stick together, the union said: none of us go back until we all go back, and they can't last forever without us.

As the days turned to weeks, the government's position took an interesting twist. No more comments were being made with respect to the strike because as far as Washington was concerned, the strike was over. A recovery program was in progress, and PATCO officially was no more. It had been legally stripped of all its powers. Business in our nation's capital—if not in its airways—was back to normal.

Having found two ways in which financial ruin can best be brought about in the shortest period of time—flight instructing and freelance writing—I started to think about other work. With considerable prodding from my equally bankrupt wife, I reluctantly thought about returning to the FAA. Every airport in the country, including Pittsburgh, needed controllers, and experienced controllers who hadn't been on strike were all but nonexistent.

Although almost two months had passed since day one of the strike, whenever I talked to my friends who had walked out, it was obvious they still believed they would be back to work before too long. How then could I, who had thumbed my nose at PATCO and the rest of the FAA, go crawling back asking for another chance? No matter how I looked at it, to do so would be betraying good friends when they needed my support the most. To do otherwise would be betraying a wife and two small children. Unlike the controllers who were fired, I had a choice in the matter, but making the right one wouldn't be easy.

In the next couple of weeks, I felt more guilt, more self-loathing, and more melancholy than I had ever before experienced. I secretly wished that I too had gone on strike so the decision wouldn't be mine to make. Yet each day's delay brought the bill collector that much closer to our door.

Having delayed the inevitable as long as possible, I made my decision. It was time to officially ask the FAA if it would take me back. I had been reasonably careful not to offend anyone when I left Minneapolis. Unless Les or someone else in Minneapolis had a personal grudge against me, the odds were fairly good that I would be rehired. I was. Within a few days of my initial request for reemployment, I was put on the rolls as a controller at Pittsburgh Tower. When forced to, the bureaucracy could move with a speed that heretofore had seemed impossible.

My first day back was far from a triumphant return to the world of air traffic control. The hour and a half that it took me to drive from my home to Pittsburgh Tower was filled with second thoughts about my decision. No matter how I looked at it and regardless of who had given me their blessing, I was still a scab. When it came down to the final moment, all my high ideals and lofty principles didn't amount to that much. I had responsibilities to fulfill, and the easiest, if not the best, way to fulfill them was as a controller. While it was just as easy to rationalize that my returning to work wasn't going to affect whether or not any of my friends would eventually be rehired, in my heart I felt otherwise. I felt as though I had gone back on my word and let down my friends, and maybe I had.

I also felt what seemed to be a very real fear for myself and my family. Strikers had never been known to be particularly fond of scabs, and I had no reason to believe my case would be any different. Although my home in Mercer afforded me the opportunity to isolate myself from all that was happening in Pittsburgh (at least I thought so), it also afforded my opponents ample opportunity to act out their aggressions. Interstate 79 between Pittsburgh and Mercer runs through little else but sparsely populated farmland. During the hours of darkness when I would most frequently be traveling on it, every overpass and every following automobile could contain potential problems.

If my imagination seemed more than slightly overactive, as I walked up the steps in the terminal building to the tower entrance, the sight of uniformed guards signing everyone into or out of the sanctuary did little to relieve my apprehensions. While similar protection for controllers' cars in the airport parking lot had been discontinued a few weeks earlier, it was clear that one or two battles still remained before the war could be declared over.

What bothered me even more was the feeling that came over me as I walked into the operating quarters at Pittsburgh for the first time. Gone were all the typical controllers with whom I had been most familiar. In their place was a collection of shirt-and-tie managers, similarly dressed staff personnel, and military controllers in uniform, all acting as if they had just retaken the Argonne Forest from the Germans. Humility was in short supply, and it occurred to me that the people I had respected the most in the FAA were now out on the street. The people I respected the least were now my co-workers.

In some ways I was right. A few seemed obviously to resent my intrusion into their private world of heroic endeavor so long after the strike, but most were pleasant if not enthusiastic.

Underneath it all, I sensed with many a superficial air of bureaucratic polish that would crumble at the first sign of opposition. The first crack surfaced when, after two weeks on the job, I told Pete, the tower chief, that I was resigning.

His initial response was, "Is PATCO harassing you?" His concern, I think, was genuine.

Actually, the complete opposite had occurred. I had discovered truth in the saying "You can run but you can't hide"—Mercer wasn't quite far enough away from Pittsburgh. About one week into my third attempt as an employee of the FAA, a neighbor and I went to Milan's Restaurant to discuss my discontent over a couple of beers. Shortly after we arrived, I thought I heard the bartender discussing the strike in general and Pittsburgh in particular with a cigar-smoking patron at the other end of the bar.

After it became clear that they were, in fact, talking about Pittsburgh Tower, my neighbor had a sudden attack of memory. He was almost positive the bartender had said something once before about having been fired from Pittsburgh. Before I could object, Frank had called him over to clarify the issue. Yep, he was right. Joe had been fired for going on strike. "How about that," Frank said. "I'd like you to meet Van. He's working down at Pittsburgh Tower now!"

The other gentleman with cigar in one hand and drink in the other was Ira. Ex-supervisor, fired PATCO controller, just-under-the-limit rehired controller, also at Pittsburgh. Somehow during my first week, I hadn't yet run into Ira at work. But from the reception I was getting at the bar, it didn't seem that Ira saw that as a huge void in his life anyway.

Talking with Joe only made me more remorseful for my recent decision, not because he threatened me with cement shoes and a rearranged nose but rather because he understood and supported my actions completely. When I told him I was thinking about resigning because of my feelings of guilt, he said I was crazy. He said that he was in the process of appealing his case, and if he won, he was going back to work immediately. The truth was he, like so many others, had never wanted to go on strike in the first place but felt that he had had no other choice.

I had to tell Pete, then, that PATCO wasn't harassing me. He could tell I was serious about leaving, and even though I hadn't had enough time to set PIT Tower on its ear with my extraordinary talent, he seemingly hated the thought of a warm body walking out the door, especially an experienced warm body. He called in the rest of the "heavies" to meet with me: Ed, the deputy chief; Bill, the operations officer; and Bob and Mal from the training department.

They all listened as I once again gave my reasons for resigning. First and foremost was the guilt, the feeling of having betrayed people I cared about and respected, but there was more. It seemed to me that people with irreplaceable experience and knowledge had been tossed aside and permanently forgotten. Many of those who remained were people who played along, people who couldn't or wouldn't try to improve weaknesses in the system if and when they saw them. The result would be an air traffic system that fostered and possibly even encouraged a sort of comfortable mediocrity. Without some of those former controllers around to help keep the FAA honest and changing, no one had to answer to anybody except someone else who felt the same as the person doing the answering.

My audience was either stunned or asleep. No one said much for a minute or two. Finally Bob spoke up. He said, "There isn't one of those fired controllers who can tell me a damn thing!"

His comment wasn't as much how he really felt as it was a symptom of the intense pressure the past few months had created, as I learned from years of working with him. I felt the others too wanted to say something, but only Bob spoke. They may have understood what I was saying; they didn't agree, however, with what I felt.

It was decided that I would take a couple of days off, think about everything that was happening, and then let Pete know my decision. In the meantime, he wouldn't say anything to the regional office in New York. If I chose to come back to work, my job would still be there. If I didn't, which he thought would be a monumental mistake, then he would have the region start processing the usual paperwork.

I did just that: thought about what I was doing, went back to work, and in a few more days left again. Pete was confused, dumbfounded, and a little angry this time, but still we parted company as two gentlemen who were on different sides of a difficult issue.

Less than a month after my return, I positively said good-bye to the FAA for the very last time, a move that all but brought an end to my eleven-year marriage. Air traffic control had seen the last of my face. It was on to advertising.

SIDE BY SIDE

TO THE MERCHANTS IN RURAL WESTERN PENN-
SYLVANIA, ADVERTISING MEANT a display ad in
the Yellow Pages. Anything more was a waste of
good money, even if you could prove that it sometimes took spending it to make it. After several
months of trying, I found out what I had suspected
all along. I wasn't a natural-born salesman or
anything even remotely resembling one.

The experience wasn't without its bright moments, however.
The small sign and advertising company I worked with had as its
staff a small group of young, energetic, creative dreamers. Together we spent hours on end in our loft-office, developing ideas that
would revolutionize how Americans looked at life. It was fun and
stimulating to sit around and brainstorm with my more artistic
colleagues, but when it came time to go back out on the streets
and sell our ideas, I stank. While we realized that it took spending
money to make it, like many of the merchants we belittled, we also
realized that it took having money to be able to spend it.

More than once I thought about my previous life as an air
traffic controller, but bouncing into and out of public service was
getting a little ridiculous, even for me. Besides, after my last
display of emotional instability, I wasn't exactly sure the FAA, and
in particular Pittsburgh Tower, would even want me again.

I was still trying desperately to figure out what I was going to do with the rest of my life when the phone rang one evening. It was Tom calling from Minneapolis. A month or so earlier I had lifted his spirits when I called and told him I couldn't stay at Pittsburgh. Sorry to hear I was out of work again, he nevertheless appreciated my support for his cause. Now he was calling to tell me what almost everyone else in the country already knew.

Word had come down from what was left of PATCO's hierarchy. The strike was officially over. It had taken more than four months for reality to finally sink in. PATCO had lost. It was time to abandon the philosophy that no one goes back until we all go back. The brotherhood-sisterhood was dissolving with unusual haste. PATCO's new posture was we're all on our own. The union leaders were already starting to use tricks and loopholes to get back to work, and if the rest of the controllers had any brains left, they would do the same thing.

Tom thought I would like to know. He also said that while he appreciated all that I had done, if there was any way I could get back into the FAA and if I still wanted to, it seemed that now would be the best time. Uncertain about his own prospects for being rehired, he was starting to look in earnest for other work. We both promised to keep in touch. We knew, though, that if I did go back to controlling, guilt would keep me from calling him, and envy or anger or a little of both would keep him from calling me.

It was decision time again. After carefully considering my options and realizing I had very few, I decided to swallow what little pride I had left and make the only sensible decision I could. A few days before Christmas, I placed one more call to Pittsburgh Tower. This time I got Ed, the deputy chief. I simply told Ed that leaving Pittsburgh had been another in a long series of career indiscretions. I fully understood that now, and if there were any way he would still be interested in having me work at Pittsburgh, I was ready to give the job the very best I had.

While I waited on the phone, Ed reported the gist of our conversation to Pete. After what seemed an interminable wait, Ed told me it was okay with Pete and him but they would have to check with the regional office before they could give me a definite answer. He told me to call back in a couple of hours. If the previous wait had seemed long, the next few hours turned into forever.

The whole thing had started out as little more than an act of desperation. I wasn't very anxious or nervous because I really thought my request would be answered with a pleasant thank-you but we don't have any openings right now. But with Christmas just around the corner, and with the strong chance to return to a job I liked more than any other, and one that also paid rather well, my hopes were higher than ever.

Finally it was time to call Ed back. When Ed came on the line he just said, "Merry Christmas. Be here Monday morning the 28th. You've got your job back."

So Christmas 1981 was especially good for me. Although I worried about the rest of my friends that day and for a long time to come, I decided that I had been given a very special opportunity, and this time I wasn't going to blow it.

If those in charge were willing to make allowances for abnormal behavior and unusual circumstances, some of the troops weren't as eager to see me return. One thing that hadn't changed after the strike was the amazing speed with which rumors spread throughout the facility. Within minutes of my departure, everyone at Pittsburgh had known why I left. Within minutes of my rehiring, just as many knew I was back.

Overall, most of the controllers and working managers were glad to have another experienced person to help share the load, regardless of my sympathetic tendencies toward ex-controllers. But a few had been so badly harassed and maligned prior to the strike that they had little use for someone who obviously thought himself worthy of extra-special treatment and who had so blatantly and recently sided with the enemy.

Shortly after my return, I was sitting in the controllers' breakroom eating my lunch when one controller, known as Gene Gene the Vector Machine, decided to let me know how he and a few others felt. With more regret than anger in his voice, Gene said, "You know there are a lot of us here who didn't want you to come back to Pittsburgh, and now that you're here we're sorry to have you."

I was a bit surprised that Gene had had the nerve to confront me so directly. I thought for a minute and then answered that I knew that was the case, and while it didn't make me feel very good, it was something that I would have to live with. I had heard that Gene in particular had been given a really rough time by the

PATCO controllers before the strike, so I knew he wasn't happy that someone he saw as a union sympathizer would once again be working side by side with him. My talk with Gene didn't make my first days at Pittsburgh any easier, but I knew I had brought most of it on myself.

The first few weeks at any new facility are at best difficult. The basic concepts are the same, but everyone and everything else is different. New controllers always tend to feel out of place and more than a little useless as they stumble around trying to match names with faces and air traffic procedures with control positions. While they're doing that, the veterans of the facility pay close attention, and they quickly, sometimes too quickly, pass judgment on whether or not the latest addition to their ranks will be an asset or a liability. Pittsburgh was no exception.

It soon became apparent that the people who had stayed behind and kept the airplanes moving over the last three or four months had become very close and supportive of one another. They weren't just six or seven crews that worked with their respective members and only superficially knew the rest of the contingent; they were a single team, working and mixing as necessary to get the job done.

With few exceptions, even the military controllers, who ordinarily knew very little about the civilian method of controlling, seemed to blend in with the rest of the team. The most notable exclusion was an Air Force sergeant that we in the military draftee ranks would have called a "lifer," a twenty- or thirty-year man. Assuming that he, not the FAA, had final authority over the troops assigned to his charge, he started sitting in the breakroom while "his men" took care of the dirty work. That lasted quite a while until one supervisor caught on.

Into his life and mine walked Ken Erb for the very first time. Like all the other supervisors, Ken had been pulling double duty as both controller and supervisor since the strike. His time in the breakroom, if he got any at all, was minimal. When he finally found out the old sarge wasn't pulling his share of the load, he decided to let him have it.

As was his custom, Ken made his comments clear and concise. He looked at the sergeant comfortably lounging on the couch and said, "Let me ask you something. Do you see any stripes on my shirt?"

Not quite knowing where Ken was heading, the sergeant simply said, "No."

"Do you know why that is? I'll tell you why. That's because there aren't any chiefs or any Indians in this building. We're all the same now. So you get your ass back in that radar room and work when you're assigned to a position, and don't let me catch you loafing out here again."

I wasn't quite sure what to make of Ken. But as a former enlisted man in the army, I did derive a certain amount of pleasure in seeing a noncom receive that which he normally dished out.

As good as the working atmosphere appeared to be, it didn't seem to help move the airplanes any better. One of my first impressions was that almost everyone working in the radar room and the tower was old, at least by controller standards. Whereas the median age had once been somewhere in the late twenties, it now looked like the mid-forties. Not that old is bad and not that mid-forties is that old, but the odds were good that most of these people hadn't worked heavy traffic in a long time.

Most of the crew were sort of checked out on the control positions, only not exactly. Some didn't feel comfortable working approach control, so they worked only departure. Some could do both but didn't want to be working traffic at all, so they worked only the positions they wanted to work. Some could work only in the tower because they just couldn't handle radar control. Others could handle only the various data positions in which actual control over traffic wasn't exercised because they weren't medically qualified. And at almost every position were two people, one to teach and another one brought in from some place or another to learn. In all, the situation best resembled a sort of controlled chaos, with the amount of control at any moment subject to change without notice.

In truth, a large part of the problem seemed to be there was usually too much control, which created an extraordinary amount of work each time an airplane arrived or departed. In the past when a pilot got the plane to the runway and was ready to go, the controller was usually ready to give the authorization. One after another they would depart three miles in trail. If the radar controller working departure control needed more than three miles of separation, he or she would use vectoring or speed control to achieve it. Within a matter of minutes the controller's responsibilities would be met and the departing airplane would be switched to the jurisdiction of the enroute center controller.

Now, there were so many restrictions that had to be invoked for each and every departure, it took two or three people to do the job one used to do. One controller—or more precisely, one paracontroller—had to call the enroute center and obtain a release time for each pilot wanting to depart. If the center said the pilot could go, another assistant had to contact the radar room to see if the departure controller was also ready for another airplane on the scope. If so, then at last the tower controller could finally clear the pilot for takeoff.

The net result was an increased work load for everyone and increased coordination among the controllers, which in turn caused an increase in confusion and a marked decrease in efficiency. Instead of three miles' separation between departing airplanes, the generally accepted norm became fifteen to twenty miles.

Since most airplane operators were back to their normal flight schedules, or very nearly so, the airplanes that weren't three miles apart in the air had to be somewhere else. Those that were in the beginning phases of their trips spent the extra time tied up in massive traffic jams at the airports. Because the fifteen- or twenty-mile spacing requirements continued through the arrival stages of a flight, the inbound airplanes more often than not congregated in holding patterns in the sky.

The result was an enormous amount of wasted fuel, continually disrupted flight schedules, and countless hours of lost time. In the controller's world where time used to be measured in seconds, and a few too many lost brought on the wrath of airline executives, I still couldn't believe the fired controllers wouldn't soon be walking through the door.

Only years later, while watching a PBS broadcast about aviation delays, did I begin to understand why the airlines had been so patient in the face of the huge financial losses brought about by the strike. Almost as a passing comment, an executive for one of the airlines mentioned that, in return for the airlines' support of the FAA's contingency plan, the FAA promised them deregulation and a fully rebuilt air traffic system within several years. Deregulation had been delivered; the rebuilt system had not.

While his explanation made the almost uncanny patience and cooperation of the airlines during those first few months after the strike decidedly more understandable, I couldn't help thinking about some of the more unlucky participants. For reasons I was only beginning to understand, the FAA's total confidence in a highly suspect and as-yet-untried contingency plan made much more sense. Without the airlines' applying political pressure for a quick resolution, time became another means to ensure the defeat of PATCO.

Although the striking controllers may have gotten only what they deserved, I wasn't sure the same could be said for the innocent victims of the strike. Dozens of small independent operators and private individuals also suffered the consequences. Many of them lost untold amounts of money and business to the extent that more than a few never bounced back. For those to whom deregulation wasn't a giant carrot dangling on the horizon, what was lost would never be regained.

In spite of what I initially perceived as a terrible disruption in service and a degradation of safety, there were also some noticeably positive changes occurring in the new FAA. With little or no time to worry about the hundreds of pages of meaningless documents that passed through the facility on a daily basis, supervisors concentrated on talking to pilots and doing whatever it took to get airplanes and passengers wherever it was that they were going. With no more time to complain or argue, controllers concentrated on the same job. So everyone ended up working side by side, together, and they achieved the goals they had set. And in a strange sort of way, they enjoyed themselves in the process.

The biggest surprise for me was how the supervisors and managers performed their jobs as controllers. Most were Pittsburgh or local tristate area natives, and many had spent their entire careers working at Pittsburgh Tower, a fact that could produce both good and bad results. On the positive side, those who had survived the rapid progress and growth of aviation over the years had been able to adapt rather well to the changing nature of air traffic control. They knew the intricacies of the airspace, the traffic flow, and the procedures better than anyone. As with most controllers who suffer the inevitable consequences of the aging process, what they lacked in response speed and recent practice they more than made up for with experience.

On the negative side, in some respects they were very much like teenagers. You could tell a Pittsburgh supervisor almost anywhere, but you couldn't tell him very much. Since most of them had little or no experience at any other major airport, there was only one way to control the traffic, and that was the Pittsburgh way. Anyone who tried even a minor variation on that theme met with serious resistance.

Each team supervisor or watch supervisor was a true character. There was Cy, one of my first bosses. I used to kid him that his favorite record album had to be "Lawrence Welk plays the best of Led Zeppelin." With his close-cropped, military-style gray hair, Cy was all elevator music and order. Even a mistake of more serious proportions would elicit only a grimace and his famous line, spoken with no more emotion than if he were making a minor adjustment to his recently placed dinner order. Cy would just look at me and say, "Well, that's not exactly what I had in mind." And then he would calmly go about righting whatever I had done that he didn't approve of.

Then there was Big Bad John. An absolute terror with some of the controllers, for some reason he never once looked at me sideways or even raised his voice to me. He was from one of the many ethnic groups that had settled in the industrial valleys of the three rivers area, and if he hadn't been a controller, he surely would have followed our ancestors who had been coal miners or steelworkers.

Rounding out the bunch were Daryl, Tom (better known to his friends and enemies as Teen Angel for his motorcycle fetish and gold necklaces), George, and Emil. They all had their own little quirks, but overall they seemed neither a particularly good nor bad force to be reckoned with. They were just there.

Last among the team supervisors was Ken. My first impression of Ken was that he was a loud-mouthed, curly-haired little guy who hardly ever stopped talking and whose abdominal protuberance seemed to indicate more than just a passing interest in alcoholic beverages. What you couldn't so easily see was his heart, which was bigger even than his mouth, and his unyielding loyalty to the controllers under his direction. Having just been severely burned by several of the fired PATCO controllers he had been a good friend to, Ken easily could have turned bitter toward those who now worked for him. Instead he became the single most important reason why my six years at Pittsburgh would be among the very best of my career.

Three watch supervisors made up Pittsburgh Tower's second

line of management, or the defense, as some higher up the line must have seen them. Robbie and Alex were interchangeable to the point that it took me several months to be able to distinguish between them. Both were always impeccably attired and groomed, and each carried with himself that certain air of dignity that said, I am *always* in control. The only way I could tell them apart was that Robbie frequently carried a copy of *Sports Illustrated* and Alex always had in his shirt pocket a matched Cross pen-and-pencil set. In the summer when the humidity was high, he used a black finish set. In the safer dryness of winter, he replaced it with a 24-karat gold-filled pair. With just the right amount of graying at the temples and the ideal height-to-weight ratio, Robbie and Alex were quintessential examples of what every civil servant should strive to be.

Then there was Joe, the antithesis of who or what the flying public secretly considered their federal mentor. The dictionary defines a Tasmanian devil as a small, ferocious marsupial having a black coat with white patches. Bugs Bunny cartoons portray it as a disheveled little creature, ferociously whirling around as it travels from one destination to another in a seemingly random pattern, only to be frustrated in its attempt, upon arrival, to determine why that destination was chosen in the first place. Whenever I think of a Tasmanian devil, I think of Joe.

Short and stocky, and always with a few strands of his salt-and-pepper hair hanging down over his forehead in defiance of the order to stay combed straight back with the rest, Joe would whirl from one radarscope to another, keeping his eye on the entire operation. Exaggerating his excess bulk were the sweaters he wore. At least two sizes too small, they either had patches on the elbows or needed them. And although he claimed to have quit smoking years ago, a lit cigarette continually dangled from the corner of his mouth. With his usual chuckle he would loudly declare, "Yeah, it's lit, but I never inhale the thing!"

While every imaginable aspect of Robbie and Alex was by-the-book, Joe's nonconformity in appearance and demeanor was exceeded by his unique method of working traffic. He always worked in the radar room, since he considered the tower beneath his rightful station. And every time he sat down to work, we all had the urge to call our families and friends to watch the airshow that was about to ensue.

Joe just had a special way with pilots. He could screw them

up worse than any other controller I had ever seen, but he did it in a way that had them laughing and thanking him before it was all over. The only thing more outlandish than his technique was his phraseology.

Because some old-time controllers saw the use of speed control, slowing airplanes down to more manageable speeds, as a sign of weakness, Joe would do it under the guise of helping the pilot and the passengers. Instead of the approved method of "USAir twenty-three, reduce speed to one niner zero," he'd say, "USAir twenty-three, for a more comfortable turn to the final, I'd suggest you reduce your speed to one niner zero." The pilots who would normally complain violently about inefficient tactics would, after Joe's silver-tongued oration, happily comply.

If he misjudged when to turn an airplane onto the final approach course, he'd still make the pilot think everything was under control. He would say, "United two eight seven, expect a tight turn to the final in five seconds." He would unkey his microphone only to have to start talking almost immediately. Although his instructions were already too late and although pilots hated tight turns to the final, for Joe they'd somehow make it all work out fine. More than anyone else I have ever known, Joe proved to me over and over that in air traffic control it's not so much what you do or say that's important but how cheerily you get the job done.

Like the blind date whose lack of desirable qualities was compensated for by a glowing personality, Joe had a huge heart. Although no one would have really wanted it, Joe would willingly and literally have given anyone the shirt off his back. Unlike several other supervisors, Joe could seriously disagree with me about a traffic problem that presented potentially serious consequences and then forget all hostility when the argument was over and we immediately returned to being the best of friends. When he finally retired, I felt as though a small but very personal piece of air traffic history disappeared with him.

Save one or two controllers left over from before the strike, a dozen or so new controllers from other facilities, and a handful of staff people, none of whom I was sure I wanted to get to know more than superficially, these were my colleagues. They could enhance or disrupt my career, and they could make my future days at Pittsburgh miserable or enjoyable. I wasn't yet sure which way it was going to go. As I looked around at all that was happening—or even more important, I thought, at all that wasn't happening—I was sure of one thing. Whatever personal turn my life took next, I would be back to normal long before the FAA and the air traffic system would be. The obstacles seemed insurmountable.

I found out very quickly that more often than not, the people who were training me to be a controller at Pittsburgh knew less about the job than I did. Not long after I started training on departure control, the easier of the two radar specialties, I entered into a heated argument with my trainer. Jack had come to the control room floor as a late-round draft pick from the data systems department, and it soon became very apparent that he had come most unwillingly. At about five feet six and no more than a hundred and twenty pounds, Jack looked no more formidable than was his approach to departure control. Everyone including Jack knew that he didn't belong in the ranks of the radar controllers. Everyone that is, except me.

I did, however, know that because of his likeable personality and even, easygoing manner, Jack was one of the favorite sons at Pittsburgh. What he lacked as a controller, he more than made up for as a person. But what I thought he lacked most was confidence, and it showed up every time he would work traffic. As soon as he sat down at a radarscope, the index finger of his right hand would instantly move to his computer entry keypack, where it would initiate a pounding assault on the "clear" key that remained incessant until his eventual relief from the position.

Were a trainee to find him or herself forced to sit between Jack and his keypack, the incessant pounding quickly gave way to continual chipping, with the trainee the new object of his all too undivided attention. On several occasions when Jack was my instructor, I dutifully bit my tongue as his nervousness repeatedly made working moderate traffic a nightmare. Finally, during one of our last sessions, when my request for a pilot to repeat a transmission resulted in a lengthy tirade from Jack on my inability to keep up with traffic, I lost my composure.

In spite of the promise I had made to myself that nothing, absolutely nothing would arouse me to the point of jeopardizing the career I had so agonizingly and so recently fought to achieve, I let Jack have it with a noticeable lack of diplomacy. Thoughtlessly and unforgivably, I did it in front of everyone else in the radar room. As the uncomfortable silence quickly settled over the radar room, I realized I had just made a serious mistake. Right or wrong, Jack was family, and I was the very new kid on the block. Making it even worse, I had just arrived from the wrong side of the tracks.

After we got relieved from the position, we stepped into the breakroom for the inevitable debriefing that followed every training session. My guess was that it would be something like "Pack your bags and get out!" To Jack's credit and my astonishment, he calmly asked me what had happened. I explained. He listened intently, made a few noncombative comments about our disagreement, offered several helpful suggestions regarding the traffic, and finished the debriefing.

As far as Jack was concerned, that was the end of it. He never again brought up the incident, and he never once used it as an excuse to attack me personally or professionally. I may have been the better controller, but I had quietly and confidently been shown who was the better man. Only years later did I learn through a mutual friend that during the Vietnam War, Jack had been involved in a heroic battlefield rescue. Because he would never talk about it, no one knew exactly to what extent his actions had helped someone else survive. Never had I misjudged anyone as badly as I had Jack.

During the remainder of my training days, there were other skirmishes with my instructors. Some were more intense than others, and on more than one occasion I again wondered who was the student and who was the instructor, but I had learned my lesson. I kept my promise to myself and for once in my life kept my mouth shut. Three months later, almost to the day, I concluded my training at Pittsburgh and became a journeyman controller. While my checkout came in almost record time, I could claim little personal credit for the achievement.

Although Pittsburgh was officially rated a busier airport, its poststrike traffic was still below what I had been used to working at Minneapolis. My transition to the big time had taken place there several years earlier, at Wold Chamberlain Airport. They were no longer around to thank, but everyone at Minneapolis Tower, even those I wanted to forget, was responsible for my success at Pittsburgh. While I realized it was time for me to put the PATCO strike permanently behind me, I couldn't help but feel tremendous regret and a sense of loss that would never completely go away.

I knew that some very good friends and very good controllers were soon to be a part of my past. I had tried to keep in touch with a few of them, but our free and easy conversations of the past had been replaced with uncomfortable, brief discussions about anything and everything except the things that were really on our minds. They had gone one way, I had gone another, and as much as we may have wanted to, none of us could go back.

A lot of the supervisors and managers were sorry too. Many openly admitted that if they could somehow selectively pick and choose the controllers they wanted back, they would gladly do it. Instead, people like Les did what they could. He helped Denny get a job as a dispatcher with one of the air freight companies. Others searched and scrounged on their own and took whatever they could find. Some sold cars, and some tried to get into other areas of aviation. A few started their own businesses, but almost without exception most suffered serious financial consequences for their actions. And no matter who you talked to or what side of the table they had been on, everyone kept asking the same questions: "How did it happen? How could we have let it get so far out of control?"

In bitterness many blamed the "others." It was Reagan's fault. He had promised support for PATCO and then backed down. It was Poli's fault. If he hadn't been so selfish no one would have been fired. It was management's fault for being so incompetent, or the controllers' for being so militant. But when the smoke finally cleared, it seemed to me it was everyone's fault. Every single person who was around at the time has to share the responsibility. Either by our actions or our inaction, we all caused the strike. As for the consequences, each of us had to accept the fact that we alone were responsible for own individual actions. As I looked around at all the new faces, I could only hope that none of us would be foolish enough to forget the past as we moved into the future.

PITTSBURGH

MY FIRST THREE YEARS AT PITTSBURGH TOWER, 1982, 1983, and 1984, held a variety of experiences and revelations, the extent of which I had never imagined possible. Events, people, and conditions changed at a tremendously rapid pace. Those crucial rebuilding years now seem little more than a merging series of wildly conceived, hardly plausible memories that randomly surface in my consciousness just long enough to play havoc with my serenity.

For more than three years I, and almost every other controller in the country, worked six days a week, every week. I watched dozens of young eager faces come and go with alarming regularity. I watched the FAA's emphasis on human relations build to a crescendo of commonly used, seldom understood buzzwords, and then just as quickly I watched it fade back into obscurity. Yet somehow, more than ever before, throughout the entire range of events and emotions that erupted in those years, I sensed that we were all a part of something special, maybe more so than any of us would ever again experience.

My first realization came shortly after the pall of training had been lifted. Through a gradual, almost unnoticeable process, I shifted from being an outsider, one of "them," to being part of the family. John was one of the first to welcome me back to their side. A typical New York City native in accent and manner, he appeared to be continually wearing a pair of those glasses that come with a big nose and mustache already attached. But when John took the glasses off, the nose and mustache remained fixed to his face.

He had come to Pittsburgh from Charleston, West Virginia, shortly after the strike began. Although he came with limited experience in air traffic control, it soon became evident that he had the talent and chutzpah necessary to become an excellent controller. When he wasn't working traffic, he approached his extracurricular antics with much the same zest and sacrilege he brought to his work. At any time anyone in the facility could become the next victim of his good-natured chiding. Anyone, it seemed, except me.

Not that he wasn't pleasant. On my return to Pittsburgh when others were still deciding whether or not they wanted me to stay, John went out of his way to be considerate and congenial. But he didn't cross the line that divides civility from the more typical controller humor until one day when he said he had something for me. Knowing that I had left the FAA behind on more than one occasion, John brought out a piece of paper. He handed it to me and said he wanted me to keep it in my wallet where I could retrieve it at a moment's notice.

When I asked him what it was, he matter-of-factly said, "It's a letter of resignation all set to go except that the date is blank. You can fill that in when you use it." Then he gave me a slap on the back and started laughing.

As I became more comfortable with the routine and the people of Pittsburgh Tower, I realized the divisiveness that was so prevalent between controllers and management before the strike had all but disappeared. Out of necessity, different teams of controllers had also become a thing of the past. Everyone simply worked with everyone else, and all of us worked together. Team supervisors and area supervisors worked side by side with controllers in both the radar room and the tower. When new controllers arrived from other facilities or the FAA Academy, we all took a turn at training them. Most of all, in spite of the heavy work load, long hours, and difficult conditions, we all had fun.

Even the pilots, whose normally scheduled lives had become continuously confounded with a never-ending series of delays, seemed able to keep it all in the proper perspective. I received more compliments, thank-yous, and words of encouragement in my first six months at Pittsburgh than I had in my previous six years as a controller. Suddenly none of us took anything for granted anymore, and each was happy that the other was still around.

In a career where a controller's excellent job performance all too often had been rewarded simply by lack of punishment, the new-found public appreciation became a strong motivator for us all. Everyone suddenly seemed to realize that the job we were doing was important and maybe not so terribly easy. More important, they frequently made their feelings known to us, and often the comments came from some most unexpected sources.

One day George, then my acting supervisor, took me aside and handed me an official-looking envelope. This kind of act was typically not a welcome occurrence for a controller. Fearing the worst, although unable to remember a transgression serious enough to warrant written intervention, I opened it. In the letter was a brief description of a recent day during which I had worked a USAir flight carrying an evaluation specialist as a passenger in the cockpit. This specialist's job was to travel around the country on different flights and rate the quality of service provided by the various controllers responsible for the planes as they operated within the ATC system.

In the past, I and many of my friends had suffered through evaluations, but they had always been in the form of oral reports passed through the facility chief to the supervisors by the evaluation specialist. *Your phraseology was correct most of the time, but you forgot to preface one call to a Cessna with the type aircraft. Your nonstandard use of "see y'all later, captain" was unprofessional and inappropriate. Basically you did a good job but there is still much room for improvement.* My letter was significantly more succinct.

Your excellent handling of traffic and obvious professionalism did not go unnoticed and Mr. Bell rated your operation outstanding.

I take this opportunity to join Mr. Bell in saying that your performance is appreciated and sets a fine example for others to follow; particularly at a time when the ATC system is under close scrutiny by the flying public.

In the months that followed, I heard that several other controllers received similar letters of praise for their performance and I was just as happy for them. It was nice to see individual effort rewarded in an individualistic way that previously had seemed foreign to the FAA. I continued to feel that way until about a year later when I received another letter for the same reason. Except for the date and the radar position I had been working, this letter was an exact duplicate of the first one. Only then did I find out that our individual efforts were being rewarded by one common form letter. While it showed little imagination and even less sincerity, I reasoned that the evaluation specialist responsible for it had meant otherwise. At least for a while, it seemed as though the FAA was changing some of its ways, and even if it wasn't, honest appreciation from even one person left me with a very good feeling.

Although increasing air traffic and our inability to move it with the same efficiency we had in the past were still a major source of frustration, other positive changes helped to compensate for our professional inadequacies. For the first time ever, nation-wide the FAA was starting to pay homage to the idea that people, not equipment, were what made the air traffic system work. As human relations took on a greater importance within the agency, the "in" phrase that passed through the lips of our most knowledgeable leaders was "People are our most important resource." It seemed to be true and it seemed to come just in time.

Our new work force was different, drastically different from those who had gone before. They were younger. Most were college educated. Many had had no previous interest in aviation. With the exception of the occasional ex-military controllers who moved into the FAA upon discharge, none of our new trainees had experienced or cared to experience the authoritarian style of management that previously had dominated both the military and the FAA.

What these young people lacked in experience and reverence for the past, they more than made up for with their enthusiasm and hope for the future. They saw air traffic control as an exciting, almost mystical career played out in the secluded confines of towers and radar rooms across the country. They recognized the security of government employment and the potential for financial independence made possible by their future salaries. But they also came with a host of new ideas about what they owed their employer and what this employer owed them in return.

For about the first two years after the strike, almost every new face that arrived at Pittsburgh Tower came by way of Oklahoma City and the FAA Academy. Because ours was a Level V tower and approach control, we received only those developmental controllers who had graduated in the top of their respective classes. Considering the fact that over half of the prospective controllers who entered the academy never made it to any facility, we received the best of the best, and they fully expected to be treated that way. Sometimes they were; other times they were not.

Under the best of circumstances, we would have been asking a lot from someone who came to Pittsburgh with no previous experience. Even though the traffic was not back to its normal pace, it was still busy and it was complex. Each controller's airspace was divided into dozens of different fragments, and no two were exactly the same. Within those sectors, varying responsibilities dictated that the controller perform a broad range of actions, sometimes separately and sometimes simultaneously. Throughout the entire operation, almost constant coordination with other controllers was necessary to ensure that the safety of each plane on the scope was never compromised. No matter what they had been told, thought, or imagined, no amount of conditioning or training really prepared our developmental controllers for the culture shock they were facing.

In many ways the biggest part of that shock was "us guys" who were already there. Although I don't know who was more surprised—us or them. Us, because they all looked and acted alike, even the women, of which there were suddenly quite a few. Or them, because the people with and for whom they now worked expected them to fit in and do the job with a minimum of fuss or confusion. We all had a lot to learn from and about each other.

The FAA, and in particular the Eastern Region, decided that the best way to teach us old dogs some of the new tricks of human relations was to send us to a seminar. Supervisors and controllers would go together and learn more about working well with our fellow man or woman. Either because we seemed to need it most or because we showed some potential for improving talents that already existed, I and my latest supervisor Ken Erb were selected to attend the first human relations seminar in Cherry Hill, New Jersey.

At the FAA's expense we would spend three days learning

how to live on the cutting edge of informed personal interaction. In spite of my inherent cynicism, the project seemed like a much-needed endeavor that deserved attention and support. If the new controllers of today were representative of the controllers of tomorrow, it was all too obvious that something had to change to accommodate their wants and needs. To some of us it was just as obvious that, to a large extent, we were the ones who needed to think about changing.

So we went. Pete, our chief; Joe, the Tasmanian devil; and Ken and I charged off to change our little corner of the FAA, if not the world. For three days we listened to psychologists, human relations specialists, and each other. We participated in workshops in which we reversed roles to try to understand more about problems the other faced. And when the formal proceedings of the day were over, we continued talking over cocktails and dinner. Although little of what we heard or did came under the heading of startling revelations, just the fact that so many of us were there gave me a glimmer of hope that the future would not be a repeat of the past.

I continued in my state of partial euphoria until about the middle of the second day. As we stood outside our conference room having doughnuts and coffee, I happened to overhear a few of the veteran FAA bosses talking. The crux of their conversation was one generally agreed-upon notion. Except for the fact that the seminar was giving them a three-day respite from their respective facilities, during which they could party, socialize, and play poker, the whole trip was a waste of time.

As the conversation rolled around to supporting future seminars planned so that others could participate, the discussion took a noticeable turn for the worse. One of the bigwigs from the New York TRACON, the facility responsible for all the traffic in what we called the metroplex area, destroyed whatever hope had been building inside of me.

He looked at the rest of his buddies huddled in their little group and said, "This has been a good chance for me to get away and screw off for a couple of days. But if the region thinks I'm going to send any of my controllers or supervisors to waste their time at another one of these things, they're crazier than I thought." His select audience members laughed, each one louder than the next, as they slapped each other on the back.

Instantly I felt as though all my time there had been completely wasted. It no longer mattered that I or anyone else might have been able to glean little bits of wisdom from the experts on stage. Regardless of what new information we would go home with, it seemed very unlikely it would ever be put into practice. Disappointed and disillusioned, I went back to Pittsburgh Tower to face life in the FAA as it now surely seemed it would always be. Tomorrow's controllers were just going to have to live with today's agency, like it or not.

Somehow, those of us who were experienced were going to have to help those new controllers make the sometimes difficult transition to the FAA way of life. The more distance we put between ourselves and the upper levels of decision makers, the easier it was to enjoy the job we were doing and the atmosphere in which we did it. Down in the trenches there were still too few controllers and too many airplanes to worry about the business of bureaucracy. Training and keeping the new controllers who arrived in Pittsburgh became more than a full-time job.

Before long, the sense of family that came from our working together toward one worthy goal gave way to a feeling of frustration that stemmed from the increasing belief that the struggle would go on forever. The agency that had promised the dawn of a new day was all too quickly reverting back to its old ways.

Nowhere was the reversing trend more evident than in the treatment of our developmental controllers, and none brought it closer to my attention than a trainee named Steve. I first met Steve when an instructor in our training department suggested that maybe he and I could carpool to work. Since he lived about halfway between my house and work, the idea normally would have made good sense.

There were two major obstacles, however, that made the idea an unappealing proposition. First, I just didn't like car pools. Second, I had tried it once before.

At the urging of the same instructor, I had taken one other new arrival along for the ride, and it turned out to be a very unfulfilling experience. When I drove all he did was sleep, and when he drove all he did was talk about how "bitchin'" his truck was. The final straw came when, one extremely dark night, he showed me how his truck could exceed a hundred miles an hour as he flipped a switch that pumped nitro into the engine. Shortly after

I ended that driving arrangement, the same fellow was fired from the FAA for his involvement in some type of illegal activity.

Regardless of how different Steve appeared, and the truth was I wasn't so sure he was all that different, I didn't want another source of irritation in my life just then. Having made my decision, I stood firm with it right up until the moment I first met Steve. By the end of our introductory conversation, everything was set. We were car pool buddies and I was a wimp who couldn't say no to anything.

After the first couple of trips together, I realized one reason why I didn't like forming a car pool. It's like walking down the street and going up to some stranger's house to ask if you can use the bathroom. No one wants to let you in for fear of the dreaded disease that may be left behind, and you're afraid that any telltale signs remaining on the sink or towels will be a dead giveaway that something in your upbringing was terribly lacking. The same seemed true in the personal domain of someone's car. No matter which side of the seat you were sitting on, when a stranger invaded that space, the first few hours were strained and uncomfortable.

After about a week of trying to figure out if smoking was or wasn't acceptable, if the ashes should be put in the ashtray or out the window, and how loud the radio should be, Steve and I began acting like ourselves. When we did, our similarities, rather than our differences, became the source of whatever discomfort remained between us. The more I got to know Steve, the more he reminded me of myself almost ten years earlier.

In his early twenties, he had already accomplished a lot of living. He was married and had a daughter, he was a skilled construction worker, he had achieved the status and responsibility of an eldest son even though he wasn't one, and he had run and lost his own business. Now it was time to move his family to a new area and take on the FAA. While it quickly became apparent he was up to the task, I wasn't sure the FAA was ready for Steve.

An ex-marine by history as well as by nature, he wouldn't back down from much. When he confronted a problem, he did it with little diplomacy and lots of emotion. Unfortunately, training was the focus of his undivided attention.

Steve was finding out that the career he had pledged himself to often meant taking one step forward and three more back. His most pressing and immediate problems resulted from the reinstatement of the crew concept at Pittsburgh. As more and more would-be controllers arrived on the scene, the practice of having everyone work together as a unit became too unruly to be effective. To no one's particular pleasure, the only answer seemed to be reorganizing seven crews, each under the direction of a team supervisor.

Each controller or developmental controller was assigned to a crew by nothing more than the luck of the draw. Some ended up going to a crew with a good supervisor and good controllers (alias OJT instructors), others got a good supervisor and no-so-good controllers or a bad supervisor and good controllers, and finally some of the very unlucky ended up with a poor supervisor and a group of controllers who were of equally questionable value. Steve's luck couldn't have been any worse.

His supervisor knew little about the correct methods of controlling air traffic and even less about effectively managing people. He was a couple of years away from retirement, and all he cared about was counting down the days until his magic moment arrived. In the meantime, as long as his crew didn't do anything to create unnecessary problems or additional work for him, they were basically left to their own devices. That included training the developmental controllers, among them Steve.

The troubles started to surface when Steve refused to accept life as it was on the crew. One of the brightest of our new arrivals and one of the quickest learners we had had in a long time, he soon realized that some of the people training him, if they belonged in air traffic control at all, most definitely didn't belong in Pittsburgh. But like their boss, whose personality they seemed to absorb through osmosis, the crew demonstrated an incompetence exceeded only by their arrogance. Unlike the more timid trainees who said or did little in their own defense, Steve wasn't of the mind to sit back calmly and let anyone else send his new career into a crash-and-burn, even if it meant upsetting his boss's well-laid plans to ride out the rising storm until retirement.

When one of Steve's trainers would correct him for doing something wrong and in fact he had been doing it right, he would let the trainer know. When the argument got heated and his boss had to step in to cool things off, Steve would let him have it with both barrels.

At one point, Steve's boss told him in no uncertain terms that he would never make it as a controller in Pittsburgh. The most logical thing he could do would be to terminate his own training and leave the FAA or go to a smaller facility. To which Steve replied, "If you want me out of here, you're going to have to throw me out!"

All the while, my job as Steve's car pool buddy was to do for him what Ron had done for another young, hotheaded controller a few years earlier. As we drove back and forth to work each day, I spent the two hours listening while the steam of fiery encounters dissipated somewhere along Interstate 79. As it did, I encouraged Steve to stay with it, hold his temper in check as much as he possibly could, and try to keep it all in perspective. Others knew he was doing a good job, and even though his supervisor threatened him with the end of his career as a controller, it just wasn't going to happen.

I patted myself on the back too, thinking I was doing a pretty good job of counseling Steve on life in the FAA. But one dark, gloomy morning as we drove to work, he told me he had taken all he could stand. He was going to punch his boss right smack in the middle of his face, kiss air traffic control good-bye, and go back to the life he knew, even if he didn't necessarily like it.

What surprised me the most was that I wasn't surprised. In spite of my efforts, I could sense Steve's building frustration, remember what it was like, and feel my own frustration for and because of him. I felt frustrated for him because no trainee should have to put up with the humiliation and degradation that too many instructors and supervisors believed was a justifiable and acceptable part of the job. I felt frustrated because of him since there was little or nothing I could say or do that would change the given order of things. I and others had tried, but in some ways our intervention had only made matters worse.

Still, I didn't want to see Steve go. Those initial uncomfortable days of getting to know each other had long since been replaced with a friendship of mutual value and trust. Besides liking him as a person, I welcomed his confidence and natural aptitude for the job. He was fast becoming one of those controllers others looked forward to working with. He knew what to do, he wasn't afraid to take a chance to get the job done, and whatever he did, he did well. His supervisor would never have been missed (and when he did finally retire, he wasn't), but we couldn't afford to lose Steve, especially now.

The rest of the way to work we talked and we argued. For mostly selfish reasons, I refused to let up on him. Just as I began to think I was making some progress, all hell would break loose: "I don't care about my career. I just want to give that old son of a bitch one good one to remember me by."

As we pulled into the parking lot, I was convinced that, if he even made it to the end of the day, this would be the last time Steve and I were going to be riding home from work together. Unlike some controllers I knew, Steve wasn't one given to idle threats. He thought long and hard about what he was going to do, but when he did finally make up his mind, that was usually the end of it.

I couldn't help wondering, after all the turmoil of recent days, how the FAA could end up almost exactly what it was just before the strike that had cost two-thirds of its work force. I knew that some people learned more slowly than others, but never did I realize that so many had the capacity to forget more than they ever knew in the first place. Or as a friend more recently put it, "Never have so many done so little for so few."

Somehow Steve did make it through that day, and many more. Although his problems didn't instantly or magically disappear, they did slowly diminish in intensity. Steve didn't change all that much. He still fought for everything he believed in, and he fought just as often and just as hard. Maybe sensing they were up against more than they cared to handle, some of the bosses, and one in particular, began to do some very fancy backpedaling. Secretly I always regretted the fact that Steve never followed through on his threat, but openly I welcomed him back to the car pool.

As Steve became a long-term resident of the tower, I frequently congratulated myself on my astute powers of intuition and judgment. Over the years he became one of the most consistently reliable, well-liked, respected controllers that ever worked in Pittsburgh. But even he made the occasional miscalculation that put an airplane where it didn't exactly belong. When that happened and someone dared to comment on his error, he would invariably look over his shoulder in dismay at the intruder and dryly quip, "What the hell, we ain't making Swiss watches here, ya know." Then back to business as usual.

Even more to his credit, when Steve's chance finally arrived and he graduated from trainee to instructor, he never tried to make the new controllers under his direction pay for what he had suffered while learning the unfamiliar world of air traffic control. He remembered what it felt like, and he knew that was one tradition he didn't want to pass along to the controllers he would train, even when some of them were the very same people who had gone out of their way to make his life miserable. It wasn't the first time that differences in individual capacities to learn had reversed the roles of instructor and student, but it was one of the few times when a situation that could have turned ugly didn't.

Most of all I was glad that Steve stayed at Pittsburgh, because I needed him as a friend. As angry as he could get at the sight of injustice, he could be just as sensitive and thoughtful whenever the need arose. He was someone I admired and respected and someone, I found, who was worthy of my unconditional trust.

For many of the same reasons that Steve struggled and faltered, other new controllers also found training a life-altering and occasionally mind-bending experience. The lucky ones fought long and hard to make it to the ranks of journeymen controllers, and their accomplishments were sometimes truly valiant. When many of us didn't think the light of comprehension would ever dawn on them, they continued to believe in themselves. When it did, they justifiably said "I told you so" and went on to become the backbone of the new work force.

While we were happy for the ones who made it through the program, there were too many more who weren't as lucky. For some it was a lack of natural aptitude that no amount of training would ever enhance. For others it was a lack of maturity, or confidence, or a little of both. I was convinced that, for most of the unlucky ones, it was a combination of antiquated teaching methods, a lack of qualified instructors, and an overall lack of management concern for the trainees as individuals.

Ironically, many of the people who should have and could have made it through the training program at Pittsburgh didn't, and some others whose lack of qualifications and ability were obvious to almost everyone but themselves did. It took more than two years for enough people both inside and outside the FAA to realize what was or, more accurately, wasn't happening, but finally the evidence became overwhelming. The reconstruction plan simply wasn't working.

There were some developmental controllers who, after a month or two into the program, displayed such a complete lack of motivation and talent for controlling that their failure was inevitable. After a year and half to two years of additional training, and sometimes great personal strain on the trainee and his or her instructors, the prediction finally came true. Again and again families suffered serious emotional disruption. Careers were drastically altered, and the number of experienced controllers at Pittsburgh remained what it had been since the strike, woefully inadequate.

As similar scenes were being repeated all across the country, frustrations over inadequacies within the system continued to build. Airlines started becoming less tolerant of the daily disruptions in service, and the controllers who had so eagerly rallied behind the noble cause of service to the flying public two years earlier were just becoming tired of the seemingly never-ending struggle to rebuild the system.

Gradually the tide seemed to be turning. As much as I wanted to ignore it, I began to get a sense of what the future might hold for us, and I wasn't especially pleased with the outlook. The response to our need for additional controllers either brought more inexperienced people from the academy or, because of budget restrictions, no one at all.

Those who did walk through the doors at Pittsburgh were given additional training time to compensate for their lack of experience and, in some cases, ability. Human relations became a topic that was addressed once every year or two when the results of the latest controller survey were released. But in general, many of us who had been around before the strike saw a significant reversal in attitudes and progress. The ghost of the future had started to look more and more like an identical twin to an apparition of the past.

KEN

MANY PROBLEMS THE FAA AND ANYONE WHO FLEW AS PASSENGER or pilot were having resulted from the very same thing keeping me and some of the other controllers happy. Almost on a daily basis, traffic in the air was increasing. Although we dealt with most of it on a routine basis, there were more than enough instances when the unanticipated, if not the unexpected, kept us coming back for more.

Except for constantly training new controllers and working six days a week as a matter of course, the remainder of life for FAA controllers returned to routine. At the beginning of each shift, arriving controllers signed in on the duty log and waded through the accumulated mounds of relevant and irrelevant paperwork in the "Read and Initial" binder.

The Read and Initial was the method of information distribution the FAA used to ensure that every controller on duty was kept apprised of the most up-to-date trends and activities occurring in the dynamic world of air traffic control. After reading page after page of who was arriving, who was leaving, and what late-breaking, imaginative new programs were being initiated by someone in the regional or national headquarters, each controller was required to affix his or her initials in the appropriately designated block. Then, if one of those controllers did or said something contrary to the policy contained therein, no one else but the errant perpetrator could be held legally or morally responsible. The number of pages in the Read and Initial binder grew at an alarming rate.

Staff and management personnel who had seen their ranks abundantly multiply prior to the PATCO strike also returned to their respective careers. Having fulfilled the task for which they were recruited—replacing the fired controllers—as new replacements arrived, it was again time for them to retreat into the shadows. With so many extra bodies fighting for office space, though, it became hard enough to find them all a room with a window, let alone something worthwhile to do once they got in it.

I remember sitting in the radar room one very snowy day, discussing the problem with the other two controllers on duty. For the better part of the last five or six hours, almost every airport east of the Mississippi River had been shut down by one of the season's biggest winter storms. While snow removal crews everywhere were using every person and piece of equipment available in an effort to keep up with the accumulation of white stuff, they all seemed to be losing the battle.

At Pittsburgh as well as the other major airports, traffic was just about at a complete standstill. Since five or six of the fourteen controllers scheduled to report for the day shift had successfully completed the trek to work, we were not swamped with airplanes. As we sat in the radar room passing time between the sporadic conversations with the few pilots who had made it into the air, one of our senior controllers made a very astute observation.

Frank, or "Old Tickets" as we preferred to call him because the "ticket" that legally allowed him to control traffic was so old that it had been handwritten on parchment paper, had been watching the endless stream of staffers moving in and out of the radar room all morning. At one pause in the parade, he looked around the uncrowded radar room, looked over at me, and said, "Do you realize there are about fifteen office people out there today working to support five controllers? I wonder if they can handle it?"

As the gap between controllers and their managers re-emerged and grew ever wider, just the opposite was occurring among the members of my (or more appropriately, Ken's) crew.

The longer we worked together and the better we got to know one another, the more we liked what we were doing and how we were doing it. Setting the standards, pace, and style of our collective personality was Ken. He was in many ways also the heart and soul of all those things crew 5 did and didn't stand for.

More than anyone else I had ever worked with or for in the FAA, Ken stood for loyalty. He expected it from those who worked for him, and in return he gave his crew that same unalterable support. If it would once again become us against them, Ken would unquestionably be one of us. Anyone who tried to get in the way of his crew soon found out that this wiry little man with the burgeoning beer belly, grayish woolly hair, and hyperactive disposition was not likely to look favorably upon the intrusion. He knew what had to be done, he knew how to do it, and he wasn't about to have anyone interfere with what he thought progress should be.

Neither was he going to let anyone do or say anything to his crew that he thought was ill-advised or inappropriate. We found that out when Wayne, one of the newer journeyman controllers on our team, got into a little bit of a bind not long after he had been checked out. In the past, after developmental controllers finished their own training, they were usually given at least a year to work by themselves before being asked to train others coming up the ladder. That year became the seasoning period during which the real learning phase of the job occurred.

It was a time that most fledgling controllers used to experiment with their own ideas, and it was a time to build confidence. If they decided during training that they would do things their own way after getting checked out, the grace period became a means to test themselves and improve their judgment. As often as not they also found there were reasons why most of the other controllers used basically the same techniques and methods to do their jobs. The ways most frequently used were the ones that worked best.

But by the time most inexperienced controllers concluded that maybe those older guys weren't so dumb after all, they had more than likely had a few "exciting" moments on the position. With no one looking over their shoulders and no one to answer the question "But what do I do now?", they had no option except to resolve the problem the same way it was created, alone. Although it could also be a time of great terror, that seasoning period, more

than any other time in a controller's life, was when confidence
finally began to flourish.

Wayne and a lot of others didn't get that opportunity to grow
up as controllers. With the shortage of qualified controllers still the
major issue confronting FAA officials, seasoning of new members
in the ranks was the last thing on anyone's mind. Particularly if a
controller was identified as having above average talent and ability,
he or she was, at the earliest possible opportunity, volunteered into
the instructor pool. Wayne was far above average in every
measurable category, and he went very early in the draft.

With little experience to fall back on, he stood behind a very
new developmental controller one busy day at the local control
position in the tower. At the same time another new controller was
training on the ground control position. Pittsburgh Tower was
operating under an East Code configuration, which simply meant
traffic was arriving and departing to the east. There was nothing
simple, however, about an East Code.

The layout of the runways and the designated use for each
piece of concrete kept the local controller extremely busy. The fact
that half the arriving airplanes had to cross the primary departure
runway on the way to the terminal added to the work load. In-
between clearing planes for landing on runways 10R and 10C and
clearing others for takeoff on 10R and 14, local control had to
respond to incessant requests by ground control to cross traffic
between departures.

Exactly where or how the ball got dropped no one could
positively say. But shortly after Wayne's trainee had cleared a pilot
for takeoff on runway 14, 1,500 feet down the runway another
airliner was starting to cross the runway. Wayne saw the problem
immediately. His quick action and the inevitable hesitation with
which today's airliners overcome the inertia of their mass allowed
an immediate resolution to the problem. The departing airliner
stopped almost before it had started to move.

Other than upsetting both pilots, both instructors, and Ken,
who happened to be in the tower observing, the incident caused
nothing more than a few bruised egos. The next day, however, the
boys in our front office caught wind of what had happened. As the
persons most directly in charge of preventing incidents, they were
instantly ready to indict Wayne for having allowed a system error
to occur.

Most of us would have judged it a system error only if the crossing airplane had not been detected until the departing plane had accelerated to near-takeoff speed. As it was, the plane preparing to take off hadn't moved any faster than a normally taxiing plane would travel. Nevertheless the preliminary steps of the investigation were getting under way.

To any controller a system error investigation can be a terribly uncomfortable experience. To someone as new to the job and as idealistic about the FAA as Wayne was, it could have easily created long-lasting side effects that might have jeopardized his career. At least that's the way Ken saw it when he arrived at work the next day and heard the news about the investigation.

Within minutes of learning of the chief's decision to reprimand Wayne, Ken went storming out of the radar room in the direction of the big man's office. Exactly what happened after he got there or what was said while Ken was in conference with the chief, none of us ever found out. But between the time he left the radar room and the time he returned, Wayne's problem had been quickly, if not so discreetly, resolved. There had been no system error, and although he had learned a valuable lesson about training, Wayne's record was still clean. As far as the rest of the crew was concerned, Ken had grown to be about ten feet tall.

My years working with Ken were deeply satisfying and enjoyable. Although he was my boss, I quickly learned he was also my friend. Because I came to Pittsburgh with a background of prior experience in air traffic control and prestrike FAA behavior, and because I was substantially older than most of the other controllers on our crew, Ken and I seemed to develop a mutual trust and respect for each other's accomplishments and battle scars. Together we also sensed that, as much as the FAA had changed in recent days, it was still very much the same organization we had originally joined years earlier.

The other thing I learned was that somehow Ken possessed the unique ability to be able to quickly defuse my occasional outbursts of anger before they got me or anyone else into more trouble than could be quietly and unofficially handled. One day when Gene Gene the Vector Machine and I were working in the tower, we got into a rather heated discussion over some not-so-trivial point of air traffic order. As the argument heated up, sarcastic comments gave way to loud voices, and by the time Ken

was walking up the stairs to rejoin us from his break, Gene and I
were nose to nose and toe to toe, ready to square off for a more
complete discussion.

Although he was slightly smaller than I and substantially
more diminutive then Gene, Ken had no choice except to step
between us and stop our ridiculous display of childish behavior.
Once he did, our tempers cooled rather quickly, and by the end of
the evening relations between us were just about back to normal.

Ken, however, wasn't so quick to forget the incident.
Realizing I felt embarrassed about my conduct, he decided to use
the incident as a learning experience for me and the rest of the
crew as well. For about the next six months, anytime Ken even
remotely suspected that I was about to get angry, he went into his
Van and Gene imitation, leaning very heavily toward the Van side.
He would puff up his chest, take a defiant stance, and dance back
and forth while all the while yelling, "Oh yeah, well take that. Oh
yeah, you take that too, sucker!" All I could do was laugh, take it
in stride, and vow never, never to lose my temper, at least while
Ken was around.

As much as he tried to hide it under a tough-guy disguise,
there was a secret behind Ken's success as a supervisor. He cared.
He really cared about the people who worked for him. If a
member of the crew was moving and needed help, he showed up
on his day off and offered his services for as long as was necessary.
If someone needed a truck, he'd toss them the keys and say, "Use
it as long as you need it. Just let me know when you bring it back."
If a new member of the crew was having trouble at work, more
than once Ken rallied the rest of the crew and let it be known that
he'd consider it a personal favor if we worked a little harder to
help that controller over the rough spots. Sooner or later everyone
on crew 5 became Ken's friend. Maybe some were a little closer
than others, but as far as Ken was concerned, we were all in it
together.

In spite of the friendship he readily offered, Ken never
compromised on performance. There was a work ethic he expected
and a standard he constantly strove to maintain. Anyone who
wouldn't or couldn't live up to his expectations, at least to the very
best of their ability, had no place on his crew.

It always hurt Ken to tell a developmental controller that his
or her calling wasn't to be a controller at Pittsburgh. Probably at

no time was it more difficult than when he had to tell Pete, a recent trainee.

For a host of different reasons, Pete and Ken had become the best of friends. It was one of those friendships that just seemed to click from the very beginning. They lived very near one another, they enjoyed many of the same interests, but most of all they, along with their wives, just enjoyed being together. If Pete and Lynn were going to dinner on the spur of the moment, after a quick phone call, Ken and Barb would be out the door to join them. If one was having a party, it was unthinkable for the other not to help in the preparation and then stick around for the fun that followed. Since Pete had sped through training in the tower and seemed on his way to becoming one of Pittsburgh's most reliable developmentals, the prospect of a long and happy friendship seemed completely assured.

Then Pete started his training in radar control. Although no one, including Pete, knew exactly why, the confidence he continually displayed in the tower deserted him from the first minute he walked into the radar room. The process through which he had so easily mastered all the necessary elements of controlling traffic from the tower instead became a daily struggle, in which he usually ended up the loser.

It was not all that uncommon for a new controller to make it through the tower training and eventually fail in the more exacting and rigorously complex arena of radar control, but no one had expected that stigma might apply to Pete. As each allotted hour of learning became a training report in his past instead of an opportunity in his future, the strain of the increased pressure showed on Pete's face and the inevitability of his future on Ken's.

It seemed as though the harder Pete tried to make it all come together or the harder we tried to help him do it, the less likely it became that it would happen. After months and months of our trying anything and everything to help, time finally ran out. As the senior controller on the crew, I was elected to be the first bearer of sad tidings.

By the time a developmental controller receives an official termination notice, it's almost anticlimactic. In most cases, rumors of a pending axing circulate for a couple of weeks beforehand, and controllers have already begun to react. The victim too has begun to sense the changes.

Once the object of irreverent ridicule that attacked anything from the illegitimacy of his birth to the lack of adequate gray matter in his head, the trainee experiences the insulation process that inevitably develops after the rumors start. As his last hours tick away, no one wants to add to the already intense pressure by saying or doing anything that might be misconstrued as another vote against his future. Consequently, instead of continually making fun of the trainee's mishaps, the controllers and other trainees conveniently find excuses to ignore them.

By the time I talked to Pete, the invisible barrier around him had become painfully evident. Everyone had quit asking him how his training was going. When he was in the breakroom, a thousand different topics of interest wound their way through the conversations, but training or future plans ceased to be included. When Pete did train, he did so with one or two specific instructors, and they spoke softly and treated him with the utmost care and sensitivity. Instead of helping Pete, though, the ritual of kid-glove treatment only made matters worse. It confirmed what he already suspected. Although he was born and raised in Pittsburgh and had deep roots in the area, if he wanted to stay in the FAA, home was going to have to be somewhere else.

I had, on too many occasions, been part of the scene when would-be controllers were told they weren't going to make it, and it was always an upsetting experience. Some took it fatalistically: if this was how it was meant to be, there had to be a reason. Others became angry and bitter, blaming anyone and everyone for their unfair treatment. More than one or two tearfully asked for more time. And some, like Pete, just felt as though they had let family, friends, and colleagues down. But the person who most felt as though he had let a friend down was Ken.

Although everyone, especially Pete, knew Ken only did what he thought was best for everyone, there was little personal consolation in making the correct professional decision. Ken felt the anguish that Pete was trying so hard to hide, and he knew that very soon Lynn would be feeling it too.

When the final day comes, most training failures, as they are called, quietly slip out the door, sometimes without so much as a thank-you from the person who had been their boss for the last year or two. Pete's efforts weren't seen as a failure, and as much as Ken might have liked to put all the hurt and self-recrimination in the past, he couldn't let Pete leave with a whimper instead of a bang.

Typically, controllers can find any number of excuses to get together and raise some hell. If there's a big football game with the local favorite on TV, it's time for a party. If it's the shortest or longest day of the year, something needs to be done to commemorate the occasion. Once in Minneapolis, the end of the shift was reason enough to celebrate at Jack's Restaurant; that celebration finally ended in Animal's driveway when the local police, with lights flashing and sirens blaring, brought up the rear of our seven-mile road rallye. And of course, there was the traditional checkout party. When developmental controllers officially finished their training and became journeymen, they were duty-bound to show appreciation to all who had helped in the struggle by throwing a thank-you bash.

Finally there was the farewell party. Almost everyone who wanted to advance through the corporate structure of the FAA had to move at least two or three times in their careers. At one time bidding points, those elusive little chits controllers needed to qualify for inclusion on the promotional selection list, were given to anyone who accepted a position in a new location. Performance success seemed to bear little relationship to the value of points a controller accrued. The FAA appeared more interested in loyalty to its policy than in the outcome of the transitions caused by them.

At any rate, we always celebrated whenever a member of our immediate crew was getting ready to climb the next rung of the success ladder. Having attended those parties as both the person leaving the facility for new experiences somewhere else and as one staying behind to hold down the fort, I knew that all of us shared many of the same mixed feelings.

While Pete's move wasn't exactly a promotion, a member of the family was leaving, and everyone on the crew, especially Ken, wanted him to know that he and Lynn would be missed, a lot. We all hoped that Rochester, New York, their new home, would give Pete the time he needed to develop what had kept him from making it as a controller at Pittsburgh, his confidence. If it did, we were sure he would be back among us before too long.

Pete's farewell party was typical of others we had thrown. The conversation shifted from work to kids to hobbies and to just about anything else that a gathering of friends might discuss. The only thing it didn't include was the reason we were there. Finally, after the cocktails, dinner, and dessert had been served, the time came to say good-bye. One by one, each member of the crew got up and spoke briefly to and for Pete and Lynn. As each new speaker finished his or her comments, the tears in their eyes became more noticeable.

Then it was Ken's turn to talk. What he said wasn't long or eloquent, but as his voice started to crack about halfway into his little speech, it became evident to all of us that what he was saying came from the heart. Later, as everyone started drifting out of the restaurant to head home, I noticed Ken saying his personal good-byes to Pete and Lynn. As I walked out the door past him, I saw that Pittsburgh's Mr. Tough Guy had tears in his eyes too.

Over the next several years my admiration and respect for Ken just continued to grow. As the FAA, its managers, and its policies continued gradually regressing toward the past, Ken kept fighting to make the lives of his crewmembers the best they could be. While other controllers were conning, conniving, and bribing to get away from the other supervisors, those of us on Ken's crew were exceedingly content to stay where we were and watch the others squirm.

Then, at long last, we believed the day was coming when Ken would be duly rewarded for his thirty-plus years of service to the government. Crazy Joe, the Tasmanian devil, was finally retiring. That meant Joe's job as area manager would be up for grabs, and Ken was going to be one of the people grabbing. The area manager is known as a second-level supervisor in the FAA. During each duty shift there are two area supervisors assigned to work with controllers. One manages the tower, the other the radar room. The area manager, to whom the two supervisors report, is in charge of the whole program.

In typical FAA fashion, the promotion to area manager brings with it more responsibility and, in actuality, less pay. But there are other benefits. The second-level manager does not control traffic and therefore need not pass the annual medical exam required of controllers and supervisors. In addition, while the area managers work the morning and afternoon shifts, they are not part of the midnight-shift staffing, a huge bonus for anyone approaching the autumn of life. But probably more than anything else, the promotion says, "Thank you. We appreciate the talent, ability, and dedication you've brought to your job."

As the job selection rumors started flying and we learned the names of Ken's competition, our spirits started climbing. Having worked in several different facilities, served as an instructor at the academy in Oklahoma City, and spent more time as a supervisor than the other applicants, Ken seemed certain to be Pittsburgh's next area manager. What we failed to consider was the fatal flaw in Ken's character.

He wasn't now, had never been, and would never be a "yes-man." Unlike some others who said only what they thought the next person up the ladder wanted to hear, when Ken's head or heart said no, the rest of him followed suit. As with Wayne's little incident, Ken had on occasion told officials that their thinking and reasoning were far from being logically or practically sound. Time and experience usually proved Ken right, and that only made his bosses angrier.

When the selection of the next area manager was formally announced, it was official; Ken didn't get the job. Since the remaining two managers were unlikely to leave in the foreseeable future, the chances of Ken's ever becoming an area manager had fallen to just about nil. Yet if he felt the disappointment and the frustration the rest of us were feeling, he didn't show it. He just continued doing what he had always done, the best job he was capable of.

During my remaining years at Pittsburgh, my friendship with Ken also continued. Although we kidded that my association with him caused my propensity for confrontation and my slipping from grace, the truth was I was responsible for my own fate. Ken may not have been seen as suitable material for an area manager's job, but two people who learned their trade as members of his crew were eventually selected to become supervisors at Pittsburgh. For them, knowing Ken was one of the best things that could have happened, and indirectly it was the pat on the back he deserved.

If anyone saw my friendship with Ken as reason to disdain me, I guess I enjoyed their foolishness. If they assumed our association was based on similarities of character, I took great pride in that assumption. If having Ken as a friend in some way disrupted my upward progression in the FAA, that climb wasn't worth the effort. The FAA gave me a career; Ken gave me whatever he had to give whenever I asked him to give it. Most of all, he gave me the gift of knowing that the next time I walked in the door to start another shift at the tower I would probably find more enjoyment and satisfaction than I had the day before. He didn't change the world, but he did change the lives of everyone who ever worked for him.

IN IT TOGETHER

WITHOUT MUCH MORE THAN A MINOR DISRUPTION TO NORMAL TRAFFIC or a temporary inconvenience for passengers, airliners unexpectedly diverted to Pittsburgh for any number of different reasons. Most of the time it was because the crew had decided a problem was serious enough to warrant shutting down one of the plane's engines. Other reasons ran the gamut from human comedy to tragedy.

Medical emergencies were almost as frequent as mechanical problems. A passenger had an apparent heart attack and needed to get to a hospital as soon as possible. Another seemed to be suffering from insulin shock or some other complication of diabetes. Still another had gone into labor several weeks early and was about to give birth aboard flight 73. Could we have an ambulance standing by? Each time we met the requests with as much assistance and cooperation as we could muster, and more often than not, the combined efforts of controllers and pilots resulted in a successful resolution of the particular problem.

While the satisfaction derived from helping save someone's life is unmatchable by any standards, it is the one-of-a-kind human experience that most quickly comes to mind. The passenger who hijacked a plane to Pittsburgh long before Pittsburgh was rated as

165

the number-one place to live ranks among the very highest on my list of unforgettable characters. After several hours of negotiations as the jet sat isolated on the farthest corner of the airport, the hijacker quietly surrendered to police, leaving us with lots of questions and no answers.

Questions also remain about my involvement with an arriving USAir DC-9. On initial contact the pilot said only that there was a serious disturbance in the passenger compartment, that he needed to get on the ground as quickly as possible, and that once there he wanted the police to meet the plane immediately. As the flight continued inbound, the pilot sporadically repeated his request and reaffirmed its urgency. When the plane finally reached the gate, our observers in the tower reported that minutes after the police boarded the stricken plane they left it with the obviously guilty party firmly in hand. We in the radar room were left to solve the riddle of the unexplained disturbance.

The ingenuity and resourcefulness of the pilots and the durability of the equipment they were flying almost always led to the same result. Incidents that, if incorrectly handled, had all the ingredients for disaster were instead met head-on and conquered with a minimum of fuss or confusion. Playing a part, however small, in any of them was one of the main reasons being an air traffic controller was so special to me.

I was only a witness, though, to the one event in twelve years that seemed most to be a microcosm of all that aviation is and all that it is capable of being. It began one evening as two military A-7 fighter jets were on a routine return flight to Pittsburgh. Having departed the airport an hour or so earlier on a training mission, the inbound flight of two was neither earlier than expected nor requesting any special assistance. Tony was assigned to the arrival south radar position and would soon be responsible for the two jets. Although one of our newer controllers, he was young, bright, and had proven himself to be completely competent. I was working that evening as his handoff controller. None of us in the radar room had any reason to suspect the rest of the shift would be anything other than busy but normal.

Suddenly Tony's already boisterous voice boomed out, "Steel 21's wingman is on fire!"

Nothing strikes as much fear into the hearts of pilots as an in-flight fire. Sitting thousands of feet in the sky surrounded by nothing but metal, air, and highly volatile jet fuel, they have few options. If there is no built-in system to extinguish the uncontrolled burning, they can only hope to land and evacuate before the incendiary prison of heat disintegrates into a devastating ball of flames.

In this flight of two A-7s, the leader in the first plane would normally control everything about the mission. Tucked in a few feet away, the wingman flying the second plane would be little more than an extension of the lead's actions. If the first plane turned right, the second followed closely behind. If the leader made a mistake that jeopardized flight safety, more than likely the wingman's future was instantly subject to an equally doubtful outcome. The pilots may have been flying two separate fighters, but as long as they remained joined together as a flight, their lives were inseparably linked to one another's.

This time, however, instead of the two pilots reacting together as one, the pilot in the crippled jet would have to break away from the leader and make separate choices. He could ask for assistance, advice, or encouragement from his partner, but his life was hanging in the balance. Right or wrong the wingman had his own decision to make.

As the event began to unfold, Tony flipped the receiver switch on his frequency selector panel to the speaker position. Until that time, everything that either pilot in the flight said had been heard only by him. It was critically important that every other controller in the radar room as well as the supervisor on duty know what was happening at the exact moment the decisions were made. Pittsburgh was operating on a "west flow" pattern, with all the traffic landing or departing to the west. The A-7s were about fifteen miles southwest of the airport, and if they chose to make an emergency landing at Pittsburgh it would almost certainly be made to the east. In both the tower and the radar room, controllers would have a lot of work to get done in a hurry. Airplanes in the air and on the ground would have to be moved out of the way of the fighters. Emergency ground crews would need to be alerted to the problem as well as to the most likely location for the planes' arrival. At the same time, the supervisor would need to direct and coordinate the activities to ensure the everyone involved was doing the right thing at the appropriate time.

Meanwhile we all listened intently as the two pilots discussed the situation and the possible alternatives. The lead pilot maneuvered his plane around the other and began describing the seeming nature and extent of the fire to his partner. The night sky made the exact origin and cause of the problem difficult to pinpoint but it provided a dark contrast to the flames coming out of the engine with ever-increasing intensity.

After a minute or two, the pilot's options had been reduced by at least one. Whatever the reason for the fire, it was not going to be resolved until the fighter was back on the ground. The question was, would the fire continue burning in a semicontrolled state or would the fuel ignite and explode before the pilot could escape to safety? And if he did try to make it back to the airport and failed, would the falling debris cause a major catastrophe to homes and towns on the ground? None of the questions promised an easy answer, but the increasing immediacy in the wingman's voice gave us all the sense that time was running out.

Then I heard something that, as a civilian air traffic controller, I thought I would never be witness to. The pilot inside the burning A-7 decided the time had indeed come to make his move. We sat waiting helplessly in the radar room less than twenty miles away from the life-or-death decision.

With little emotion to compare to the immensity of his decision, the pilot said, more to his flight leader than to anyone else, "I'm going to eject."

All of us listening were stunned. It wasn't that we felt he was making the wrong decision. We recognized the courage it must take to stay inside a cockpit that could instantaneously disappear without the slightest warning, and many of us wondered why it had taken him this long to decide to punch out of the fighter. Still, the thoughts of what might happen as the pilotless jet fell uncontrollably into the darkness below were frightening.

No less upsetting was the idea of its pilot parachuting equally helplessly down to the hostile terrain of foothills, trees, and power lines below. I had once briefly entertained the idea of jumping out of an airplane in the daytime, under almost ideal conditions with plenty of expertise to guide me, but had chickened out in the name of sanity. I could only begin to imagine what this pilot was about to face.

As the pilots started to increase the distance between their two planes in preparation for the bailout, the leader told Tony what the plan was. Although the sparsely populated area beneath the jets offered little light to help the pilot pick the spot in which the jet would ultimately crash, he wanted to try and put it into the Ohio River just along its banks, thereby lessening the chances of hitting anyone or anything on the ground. When the wingman left his plane, the leader would tell Tony of the exact moment. Tony or the supervisor would then mark the exact spot the target was last seen on his radarscope with a grease pencil. If some type of air rescue became necessary, that mark on the scope would enable controllers to direct air crews to the precise location of the crash and the pilot. With all the preparations completed, we waited, listened, and watched as the target on the scope moved into position near the river.

Then the word we had all been waiting for finally came through Tony's speaker. "He's out!" the lead pilot said.

Pilot and plane had instantly and abruptly separated. All anyone could do now was wait and hope that the pilot would survive the nighttime ejection and that the pilotless A-7 would reach its final resting place without harming anyone or anything along the way. As we quietly waited for the answers to some of our questions, given the odds of the situation, it seemed we were asking for an awful lot.

Although he would very soon be running low on fuel, the leader of the now defunct flight of two continued to circle the location where he last saw his partner alive. If the other half of the team did make it to the ground safely, a hand-held radio in his survival pack would enable him to communicate with the airborne pilot. If no transmissions were received from below, the leader at least wanted to stay in the area as long as possible to help direct crews to the crash site.

Finding the downed fighter even in a relatively unpopulated area would be a lot easier than finding an injured pilot, especially if his injuries prevented him from helping rescuers narrow down their search. Knowing how helpless those of us in the radar room had been feeling since the beginning of the incident, I could only imagine how painfully inadequate the pilot in the surviving A-7 felt as he watched from above. From the start of their mission's preflight briefing many hours earlier, the two pilots had acted in harmony as a single unit. They had taken off side by side, achieved their objectives as a team, and until a few minutes earlier had fully expected to taxi back to the Air Guard Base as leader and wingman. As close as they had been, now they were two very different individuals with only limited ability to help one another.

We first learned the location of the crashed A-7 when the flight leader relayed his estimate of where the site was. Even though anyone within a few miles of the impact point would have no doubt seen or heard something, we passed along his information to local and state authorities in the general area. Whether the jet had caused injuries or damage to people or property on the ground, however, couldn't be determined from the air. For that news all of us would have to wait still longer.

Then, as eavesdroppers, we heard the first good news of the evening. The flight leader yelled, "All right, you made it! That's terrific, that's just great!"

For the next several minutes we listened as the pilot flying overhead first sought and then relayed vital information from his teammate on the ground. The downed pilot was too far away from our antennae for us to hear his answers directly, but from the side of the conversation we could hear it quickly became apparent his escape from the burning A-7 had been a resounding success. In parachuting to relative safety, the pilot had sustained what felt like nothing more than a few minor injuries. He was, however, most anxious to be evacuated from his present surroundings and transferred to a more hospitable environment.

His friend circling above just laughed and said, "Don't you worry. I'm going to have to leave soon, but help's on the way, I promise."

From what we could sense as well as hear of the one-sided conversation, save for one happy man on the ground, no one was more relieved at that moment than the pilot of the remaining A-7. As flight leader he was responsible for everything that happened until the mission was over, and his mission wasn't over until everyone involved was back home safe and sound. While the other half of the team was apparently as safe and sound as could be expected under the circumstances, he wasn't yet home, and his mentor wasn't at all happy about having to leave him before that was accomplished.

But unless he wanted to face the prospect of not having enough fuel to return to the airport, he couldn't wait around until more help arrived. Like it or not, he would have to break communications with the stranded pilot and leave him alone to wait. But the A-7s weren't the only ones flying a sortie that night. Almost as if by design, a returning Air Force C-130 Hercules cargo plane had been monitoring the frequency for the last few minutes, and upon hearing of the flight leader's inability to remain on the scene, its crew volunteered to take his place as spotter and communications relay.

Because of the nature of their missions and the planes they flew, fighter pilots quickly became accustomed to measuring their remaining time in the air in minutes. The four-engine turboprop Hercules, though capable of flying at only a fraction of the speed of the more aggressive fighters, had proven itself to be extremely effective and reliable as a transporter of people and equipment in some of the most hostile conditions imaginable. Unlike the A-7s, the C-130s could measure time in the air in hours.

Feeling a little more confident that he wasn't abandoning his wingman in some unpardonable way, the flight leader left his friend in the hands of a new but equally concerned team of guardians. At almost the same time, one of the local hospitals that provided air ambulance services for the Pittsburgh area had dispatched a helicopter to retrieve the waiting pilot. Though the C-130 crew's most valuable function may in fact have been to offer moral support and camaraderie to the waiting pilot, they now would also be able to help direct the helicopter to his exact location.

When the helicopter first contacted our approach control for vectors to the expectant passenger, we knew that we too were becoming more directly involved with the rescue. We just didn't know how complicated it was to become or how much in the middle we would end up being. The operation started out to be as routine as picking up a pilot who had just ejected from a burning jet could be. For us it was a matter of providing the helicopter pilot with vectors to the point on the radarscope where the C-130 was circling. When he got there, our job would essentially be over. The pilot on the ground, the crew in the C-130, and the helicopter rescue pilot could together pinpoint the precise location on the ground where passenger and helicopter would meet for the trip back.

Just when we thought it was time to sit back and relax, unexpected events started to unfold. Apparently unable to talk to his helicopter pilot directly, the hospital director for whom he worked called the radar room and asked our supervisor to relay a message: Under no circumstances was the pilot to land the helicopter anywhere but on an approved landing site.

We didn't know exactly what constituted an approved landing site, but we figured that the odds of the A-7 pilot's ejecting over and parachuting into one were small enough to create a significant delay in his rescue. Still, we had no choice but to pass along the information to the hospital's helicopter pilot.

What I remember most about the next few minutes of the rescue attempt is a lot of confusion. Being the moment we had been working toward since the beginning of the incident, it should have warranted our complete attention. Yet somehow that call from the hospital seemed to muddle all the issues. I remember the C-130 crew directing the final movements of the helicopter and various conversations—between the downed pilot and the C-130 crew, the C-130 crew and the helicopter pilot, the helicopter pilot and our approach control, and the pilot and the helicopter pilot.

I remember confusion as the helicopter pilot tried to get us to confirm that he had received our message from his director correctly. It didn't seem to make sense to him. Apparently he had landed in other similar areas before and couldn't understand why this pickup should be considered different. Adding to the confusion was the fact that the A-7 pilot could see he was within minutes of being taken aboard and didn't understand the delay. All the while we were trying desperately to reconfirm the original message and at the same time obtain an explanation for the rescue pilot.

To those people back in the hospital's executive suite, the question of liability seemed to be the most pressing issue. To the players trying to use sound judgment in a situation filled with a real sense of immediacy, the decisions didn't seem to be black and white but rather varying degrees of obscure gray.

When we did finally obtain reconfirmation that the original directive was correct, the pilot in the helicopter seemed unable to hear or understand what we were saying. Whether he had dropped below the altitude from which we could effectively communicate or his radios developed problems, we were never exactly sure. What we did understand was the next time he came back on the frequency, his helicopter had one additional person on board, an errant A-7 pilot.

Almost as quickly as we breathed that final sigh of relief, life in the radar room returned to business as usual. Other than a brief rehash of the evening's events by one or two of the controllers, it was as if the entire incident was nothing more than a momentary interruption in an otherwise routine shift.

The typical banter that was an integral part of our repertoire, however, was conspicuously absent. Instead, each of us seemed content to reflect on what did happen, what didn't happen, and what could have happened, in our own individual ways.

As the last departure rush of the evening was winding down and I was about to say good night to one more airline captain heading out for his last trip of the day, he and I had an exchange of transmissions that, however brief or terse they may have sounded to an outsider, somehow put it all in perspective for me. Evidently he had been on an inbound flight at the time the A-7 caught fire and had heard at least part of what was happening. But since communications with military pilots normally take place on the UHF radio band and not in the VHF range used by civilian pilots, the pilot with whom I was now talking had been able to hear only Tony's responses to the crisis.

Still, he had heard enough to know that the developing incident was critically serious. One person's life was hanging in the balance, and the potential for more widespread destruction was a very real possibility. As much as this captain might have wanted to stay in the air to offer assistance, he must have realized his efforts would have been futile as well as imprudent.

Yet for some reason, either because some of the A-7 pilots were personal friends or just because they were fellow airmen who shared many of his same risks or concerns, the captain had been unable to forget the transmissions heard earlier in the evening. As he was about to leave my frequency and contact the next controller down the line, he asked about the plight of the pilot in the A-7. I gladly told him that the pilot was safe and that, as far as we knew, the crashed fighter had caused little damage and no injuries to anyone on the ground.

He answered, "Ah, that's just wonderful! That kind of news just made the rest of my evening perfect."

The obvious pleasure in his voice would have been all but impossible to conceal, but then why shouldn't it be that way? I knew exactly how he was feeling.

CONSCIENCE AND DÉJÀ VU

THE EVENTS SURROUNDING THE CRASH OF THAT A-7 LEFT ME feeling incredibly proud and fortunate to be part of a group of men and women who seemed to have a true understanding of the uniqueness and value of each day. I began to feel frustration in equally large doses, though, whenever I saw the lack of those same qualities in the people who were calling the shots for us all.

Whether it was the airline executives who scheduled thirty or more departures at the exact same time, knowing only the first two or three would actually leave on schedule, or the bureaucrats in the FAA who said, "If that's what they want, make it happen," common sense and sound judgment seemed to take a back seat to politics and economics. In the process, people became an expendable component of the system, and others too felt the frustrations.

As the hub-and-spoke program initiated by the airlines gained momentum and the number of daily flights into or out of the nation's major airports steadily increased, pilots and controllers alike began to feel added pressures. Tired of the constant delays and almost continuous disruptions to normal schedules, pilots routinely became more and more agitated with the controllers, who bore much of the burden for their dissatisfactions. Controllers tired of trying to cram 1980's volume of airplanes into 1950's capacity airports started to get fed up with the system as well. In the meantime, almost everyone else involved with or affected by the air transportation system started putting pressure on anyone they could think of who could make it all better.

In response, the political machinery of the FAA, which had lain dormant for several years after the PATCO strike, oiled its aging parts and shifted into high gear. Those most often caught on the spinning treadmill were pilots and controllers.

On the national level, public pressures were first felt by congressional representatives, who passed them on to FAA officials, who in turn redirected them to controllers and supervisors in the field. New policies created additional problems for an agency already struggling with the rapid growth of air traffic. As the FAA's plan for rebuilding its work force after the PATCO strike dragged years beyond what had been originally anticipated, Congress finally presented it with an ultimatum of sorts: Increase the number of journeyman controllers to somewhere around 75 percent of the allotted staffing or face the prospect of hiring back at least some of the fired controllers.

Although many working controllers saw the prospect of adding experienced applicants to their stagnant numbers as anything but dim, others in the FAA weren't yet willing to concede that the time for such drastic action was at hand. Instead, controllers who were already providing developmental controllers with three or four hours of on-the-job instruction almost daily would increase their efforts as once again a new emphasis was placed on training.

Along with that new emphasis came a not-so-subtle shift in expectations. It soon seemed as though the standards expected from the next generation of controllers might be different from those used in the past. If they couldn't make it through the program as it existed, and if the number of replacements for those who failed was inadequate, it was time to change the program. It was time to give those new controllers who had received the prescribed instruction but weren't able to demonstrate competency in their duties additional time to meet the minimum standards of the job.

At best our reactions to the new guidelines were mixed. Having more than once seen policies that seemed sound and reasonable at the outset end up being twisted and altered beyond recognition by lower-level managers clawing their way to the top, this new outlook on training foretold worse things to come. While there were most definitely a few borderline developmentals for whom additional training time could mean the difference between success and failure, for many more the extended training would only delay the inevitable.

While none of us particularly looked forward to the task of spending more time training developmentals in a career for which they might have at one time been deemed ill-suited, the added work load was but a minor consideration. At the heart of our concerns was the possibility that relaxing some requirements might be misconstrued as an implied approval to bypass other standards of long-standing tradition.

Even before the dust had had a chance to settle on the new regulations, our worst fears began to be realized. In the past, the controllers who had provided developmentals with the majority of their training had always been given the opportunity to be the very first to recommend them for certification on each of the control positions. That policy was a courtesy to the individuals who had given so much of themselves to the new controllers, but it had a more tangible purpose.

The final certification of a controller comes when a supervisor formally and officially administers the checkride. Trainee and supervisor both plug into the control position, and for the next hour or so the would-be controller performs at the highest level possible. If a few minor mistakes are made, and usually there are at least a few, the supervisor evaluates them in terms of the controller's overall effectiveness. If the safety of pilots or passengers is never compromised, the trainee walks away from the session as a checked-out controller. If not, he or she receives additional training and then does the same thing all over again.

In reality, by the time a developmental controller gets to the checkride, the decision has already been made. Throughout the months-long training, instructors have continuously evaluated both progress and performance, and supervisors rely—at least they used to—on an instructor's recommendation before initiating a checkride. As good or bad as a developmental may be on a particular day, it is impossible to examine or determine consistency of performance. For controllers, inconsistency can be just as dangerous as having no ability at all.

But as the congressional deadline came closer and closer, an insidious change in thinking became more and more apparent. With increasing regularity, marginal controllers who one day seemed unlikely to ever succeed in training were the next day added to the list of journeymen controllers. Their instructors' recommendations, or lack of them, were ignored, overlooked, or never even sought. When it was all over, those same controllers were added to another list—a list that sentenced them to work with ever-present knots in their stomachs and doubts in their minds. Making it worse was the feeling that the controllers with whom they would work shared the same doubts about their ability to get the job done.

On the local level, pressure from users of the air traffic system came in more direct and immediate ways. Our main customer was USAir, and as a result of its influence, we were forced to answer to the company in ways that sometimes seemed incompatible with the supposed independence of a federal agency established for the benefit of all segments of the aviation community.

Although a national tracking system known as Central Flow Control is supposed to monitor, predict, and react to bottlenecks in the air fast enough to prevent the wasteful practice of holding (circling airplanes over designated areas until congestion is relieved and the flights can continue as originally planned), it doesn't always work. For any number of reasons, including unexpected bad weather, accidents that close a much-needed runway, or the lack of controllers needed to staff all the necessary positions, unanticipated holding can and still does occur.

Regardless of the reasons for holding, when it happens without the express, written consent of Central Flow, the timing so critical to the success of the hub-and-spoke system starts to break down almost immediately. When it does, passengers become delayed and disgruntled, and the potential for a loss of revenue by an airline increases dramatically. All of this makes the decision to hold airplanes a universally unpopular one.

Even the controllers who initiate holding aren't happy about having to make that choice. Delaying airplanes in the sky doesn't make less work for anyone, especially controllers. Instead of quickly and smoothly moving everyone through the system to their destination, holding creates huge bottlenecks, the repercussions of which are occasionally felt throughout the entire nation. Sooner or later, even if it's much later, all those airplanes that were held still have to get where they were originally going, and the controllers who held them are usually the ones who finish the job.

Why then hold in the first place? It's a matter of judgment and safety. If circumstances at an airport reduce the number of planes that can land in a given hour but those planes are already in the air converging on the airspace around that airport, the approach controller runs out of places to put the traffic. With more coming into the airspace than are leaving it, and with each one traveling at least four miles a minute, a lot of pilots end up with no place to go and they get there in a hurry.

Although holding is not a favorite pastime among pilots, they understand that it is one of the necessary evils of big city life. Airline executives, however, do not. Without exception, whenever we initiated holding and any of USAir's fleet got caught in the crossfire, the phone in the radar room would ring within minutes of the first delay. At the other end of the line would be an FAA representative in Washington wanting to know what the reason was for the delays. Having had his cage rattled by someone from USAir's headquarters, also located in Washington, he wanted some answers.

Within seconds of that call the inquisition would work its way through the area manager and the area supervisor down to the controllers. At that point it often intensified. Why did you start holding? Can't you take a few more airplanes? How long are you going to hold? With each additional question came the inference, if you can't handle the traffic we'll get someone in there who can. Of course, every controller in the radar room understood the reason for the hold, and each would have done exactly the same thing. The added pressure was unmistakable, unwelcome, unnecessary, and very poorly timed.

Almost daily, in subtle, imperceptible ways the divisiveness that had pervaded much of the FAA before the PATCO strike started to return. The us-against-them feeling that pre-1981 controllers remembered only too well was again becoming a common topic of conversation in the breakroom. In the midst of it all, the FAA decided to add another element to the problem. Mandatory drug testing for all controllers was about to become reality.

The assumption was that since controllers as a group were representative of society in general, and since drug abuse was becoming more and more prevalent within society, drug abuse also had to be a problem among controllers. An answer to the problem had to be found.

While only naiveté would have allowed us to believe that drug abuse wasn't a problem for any of our friends, widespread implementation of a program to deal with singular abuses not only clouded the more significant issues affecting safety in the system but punished everyone for the mistakes of a few. It seemed also to drain valuable resources and attention away from areas more immediately in need of attention and waste them where they were needed the least.

Of all the controllers in Pittsburgh, two either had a substance abuse problem significant enough to affect their job performances or else they were just inherently incompetent. Most of us suspected the former, but either way the results of their controlling tactics were so blatantly inferior that something had needed to be done long before drug testing came up. When the testing program finally did document the already obvious, one got caught and was eventually released from the FAA; the other turned out to be just incompetent and is still on the job. By government standards, that probably made the program a resounding success; by most controllers' standards, it left the real problems still waiting in the wings.

Not being addressed were all the rest of the concerns that plagued controllers on a daily basis. The amount of on-the-job training required by journeymen for developmentals seemed to be increasing. As fast as new controllers were added to the ranks of the fully qualified, their seniors moved on to new and different positions away from Pittsburgh. The result for those left behind was almost always a net loss of experience that translated into a net increase in expected effort.

As our numbers either stayed the same or decreased, traffic continued to build. With each new added flight, the inbound and outbound rushes became more and more unmanageable. Using the same airspace, equipment, and procedures that had been in existence for more than twenty years, the FAA answered the call with stop-gap measures. Combine two control positions on the departure control side of the room and move one of those controllers over to the busier arrival side to help. Eliminate training the new controllers who will eventually reduce the staffing shortage and send them to work in the tower. Take just two or three more airplanes and then hold, but only as a last resort.

With each new day, controllers who had been working six days a week for three, four, or five years just got more tired. The light at the end of the tunnel started to disappear, and with it went the hope that somehow things would eventually get better. I started to get an increasingly distinct feeling that I had been in this situation before, and my best recollection was that I hadn't liked it.

Evidently, more than a few others felt the same way. Surprisingly, many of the discontented controllers were people who hadn't been part of the prestrike FAA. Their displeasure with the current state of affairs was based only on events that had occurred within the past four or five years.

The voices may have been different, but the words they were saying still sounded awfully familiar. This time, however, they had a couple of officially sanctioned government surveys to confirm that many of the complaints they were airing were not just the concerns of a few isolated malcontents. In spite of the fact that more than 90 percent of the controllers surveyed found the actual job of controlling traffic to be completely satisfying, more than 50 percent were dissatisfied with supervisory and management practices within the FAA.

For almost all of the controllers who responded, money wasn't even an issue worth mentioning. They were content with annual paychecks that regularly exceeded fifty thousand dollars. Nevertheless, the host of twenty-three- and twenty-four-year-olds who made up the majority of the FAA's new work force had begun to feel the frustrations of working for a management system that increasingly seemed unresponsive to their needs as both controllers and individuals.

Tired of hearing answers that didn't seem pertinent to the questions they were asking and tired of seeing little if any changes for the better in their day-to-day working environment, the new generation of controllers looked to the past for a solution to their problems. The result was NATCA, the National Air Traffic Controllers Association. Less than six years after the demise of PATCO, in a profession where they least belonged, once again the lines between labor and management were being clearly drawn.

As PATCO had in the very early days, NATCA leaders gained members by saying theirs was to be the voice of concern and safety, not argument and strikes. They reasoned that if the FAA would not listen to individual voices straining to be heard, then the only alternative was to combine them into one united voice that couldn't be ignored. Sadly, as much as many of us hated to see the return of an adversarial relationship between controllers and their managers, there didn't seem to be any other choice. The truth was the division between the two groups had been in existence for some time. The emergence of NATCA only served to formalize the alienation controllers had already begun to feel.

With each new turn of events, I felt a strange combination of bitterness and despair. More than eleven thousand controllers had lost their jobs permanently. Airlines had lost huge sums of money. Air travel had been disrupted for years. An entirely new work force of young, energetic, motivated controllers had been recruited and trained. And all we really had to show for it was an agency for the future that bore an uncanny resemblance to its forerunner.

Intellectually I had promised myself that if I ever saw a return to the ill-conceived ways of that past, I would fight it every step of the way. Emotionally, as I began to see that nightmare develop, I sensed that my personal battle had already been lost. If eleven thousand jobless faces weren't enough to remind the FAA of its lack of concern for the very people it showcased as "our most valuable resource," it seemed highly unlikely that one or two or three of us could become the conscience that was so obviously missing.

Still, some tried to do the impossible. But those who fought, no matter how valid their motives, only antagonized their opponents. That impersonal bureaucratic wall, so recently knocked down by events surrounding the PATCO strike, had already been reconstructed. Anyone caught chipping away at its authority now was surely an enemy who belonged on the outside of it, and anyone foolish enough to support that offender was equally unwelcome.

For reasons I neither chose nor refuted but simply found myself believing in, I somehow ended up on the outside looking in. With me were a few I was proud to be among. Besides Ken, Steve, and one or two others, there was Charlie. An ex-navy controller and an ex-trucker, Charlie was physically more than anyone at Pittsburgh Tower cared to confront openly. All too often they instead attacked him from behind, and more than once Charlie and I found ourselves fighting back-to-back just to protect each other. Charlie was someone who put principles and other friends high on his personal list of priorities.

As much as he and I enjoyed playing the role of devil's advocate, I knew that our comments would ultimately change little. The only thing that changed was the one thing that had, up until now, kept me coming back for more. In all the years of controlling, I had valued most my extreme good fortune at having stumbled into a career that never failed to provide me with a tremendous sense of satisfaction and accomplishment. I loved the job I was paid to do. Somehow, that had changed.

I still loved the job, but I found myself more concerned with other issues. Many seemed so all-consuming that little else I did erased their importance. And most issues seemed so uncontrollable that whatever I did, it wasn't enough. A picture in my mind started to develop, and I didn't especially like what I was beginning to see.

I thought about events and people from the past and realized that the very ones I liked the least were becoming a part of my life. I had to somehow change either who I was turning into or the environment in which I was letting it all take place. Having vowed to never again let anyone or anything run me out of a career I wanted, I felt a flood of emotions come pouring back into my head. I didn't want to leave and I didn't want to stay. As the thoughts raced through my mind, I realized that I, too, had come this far only to be facing the same problems I had run away from a little more than six years ago.

It seemed that in my righteous indignation, I was only too willing to condemn others in the FAA for the same faults I was guilty of. I wasn't convinced that anything would make much of a difference, but in my stubbornness I wasn't convinced that I shouldn't try. It may not have been the most optimistic way to look toward the future, but for the time being it was a lot better than using the letter of resignation John had given me several years earlier.

LAST HURRAH

IT TOOK ME MORE THAN EIGHTEEN MONTHS TO
MAKE A DECISION I thought was sound enough to
live with. During that time, my emotional pendu-
lum swung back and forth more wildly than at any
other time in my life. One minute I was at the very
pinnacle of professional satisfaction, only to find
myself plummeting into the abyss of personal
despair the next. In-between, in my most lucid
moments, I tried to make sense of it all.

My greatest satisfaction stemmed not from controlling but
from my writing efforts. After almost ten years of trying, I saw my
first article published in *Flying* magazine. The year culminated with
a phone call from the magazine's executive editor, Nigel Moll,
offering me my first assignment as an official contributor to the
magazine that, to me, represented the very best of aviation
journalism. I felt I could ask for little more.

At the same time I was blessed with the good fortune of
seeing one of my discarded projects become another dream
realized. As I carefully nursed it through review and revision I witnessed one of the most amazing and satisfying transformations of
my life: what had begun as nothing more than a set of ideas moved
first to a stack of poorly typed, double-spaced papers, changed into
a set of proofs, and emerged as my first full-length published book.

Even my daily frustrations of working for an agency prone to either stagnation or regression were overshadowed by occasional recognition of my professional abilities. Regardless of the obscurity or the unintentionality of those gestures, they nevertheless gave me cause to be happy.

For reasons I hoped were directly related to the amount of time and effort I had spent trying to master my craft, I was chosen to participate in a couple of different events. The first was related to President Reagan's upcoming visit to Pittsburgh. Although controllers in the Washington, D.C., area routinely provide air traffic services to Air Force One, the airplane in which the president travels, without unusual fanfare or regard, the same is not necessarily true in other areas of the country.

The opportunity to share with the chief executive his national limelight, if only for a moment, brings to the hearts of budding bureaucrats a mixture of excitement and concern—excitement because most of the community will be watching their airport on the evening news, concern because one of their controllers might screw up and endanger or at the very least inconvenience their leader. However elaborate or extensive, any precaution that could be employed to reduce the chances of such a mishap would be used.

Controllers, however, viewed the occasion from a slightly different perspective. We knew that every manager from the top down would be in either the radar room or the tower watching every movement of the controllers on duty with a suspicious eye. We also knew that normal traffic would be disrupted or delayed until the presidential plane was safely parked on the ramp. The president's arrival, then, was not necessarily reason enough to break out the party hats and streamers. But as much as I believed that the president should receive neither more nor less than anyone else who flew into Pittsburgh, I still took pride in knowing I had been picked to help make his trip a little safer.

The other event that gave me an opportunity to contribute, though less publicized than the president's visit, was more formidable. After more than two years of slow materializing, at long last our new home was ready to inhabit. The new tower, all 227 feet of it, the tallest FAA-constructed tower in the country and the flagship of the fleet, was about to become operational.

The cutover would begin during the evening of March 12 and

continue into the early morning hours of March 13. Sometime between 11:00 P.M. and 6:00 A.M., the lines that for more than thirty years had supplied the old tower with all its vital radar and communication links would be physically severed. For a brief period of time, the controllers at Pittsburgh approach would have to conduct business with a limited number of radio frequencies and no radar. If the technicians responsible for the cutting, splicing, and transferring were successful, the new Pittsburgh approach would be on-line and operational before the next morning's 7:30 rush of inbound planes developed.

If something in the changeover went awry and things didn't go according to plan, there would be immediate problems to resolve and we would not be able to go back to the old tower or radar room. Once the surgery was under way there could be no turning back. We would have to do our best with whatever we had that did work.

As the only controller in the new radar room, I had the job of waiting until that moment when the months of preparation would be put to the test. Having survived two other modernization programs at Toledo and Minneapolis, I hoped for the best and expected the worst. We ended up getting a cutover that was somewhere in the middle. At 3:52 A.M., an air cargo pilot flying Don Juan 501 became the first person to receive service from the new radar room. At about 7:00 A.M. our radar become operational enough to meet the needs of the day's traffic. At about 7:45 A.M. I left the building, tired but satisfied. However small my individual contribution, I was proud to have become a part of the legacy of air traffic control and prouder still to have been asked.

But of all the goals I was able to reach, there was one that still lay just beyond my grasp. As hard as I had tried and as much as I had wanted to make it happen, I had so far been unable to graduate from the ranks of controllers and become an area supervisor. In the past two years I had bid three times on supervisor jobs at Pittsburgh. Each time another applicant had been found either better qualified or more suited for the job, and each time I felt the resentment within me grow a little stronger.

Of the three, I thought only one was really more qualified than I to fill the role of area supervisor. Dave had come to Pittsburgh after serving as a controller at Washington National Airport and as a supervisor at Clarksburg approach in West

Virginia. Besides being an excellent controller, he had a genuine concern for anyone who worked with or for him, and I was certain that neither quality would fall prey to his future ambitions. Of the other two, I couldn't say the same.

They did, however, display qualities that were either not in my nature or ones to which I couldn't subscribe. Both were team players who enthusiastically supported each and every edict handed down from on high. Whenever a reinterpretation or a misinterpretation of policy necessitated a change in thinking, both were able to diplomatically and quickly change their opinions and postures. I was convinced that, if the need arose, both would sacrifice anyone who happened to be available.

Those most often available were controllers, and the opportunities most frequently used were altercations or incidents within the system. Depending upon whether it was a pilot or a controller who initiated an investigation, the premise under which the inquiry was launched changed significantly. Any pilot accused of erring was innocent until proven guilty. Any controller called on the carpet to explain was most definitely guilty until proven otherwise.

Although my own past experiences did not wholly substantiate those tenets, I was about to learn that the fundamental truths by which they were established were only too valid. My awakening came on the heels of an incident that involved the captain of a USAir 727, an A-7 fighter, and me. The two aircraft were both inbound for landing at Pittsburgh, and I was working at the arrival south radar position.

The A-7 was one of a four-ship formation flight, but the pilots of the other three jets escaped the incident unscathed. The weather was nearly perfect as the pilots in the A-7s and the 727 prepared for the final phase of their respective flights. The plan was for the A-7s to make an overhead approach, during which they would fly directly over the runway in formation and then, one by one, separate from the flight, make a tight circling pattern, and land. After that the 727 pilot would fly a visual approach and, using his visual sighting of the airport for course guidance, land on runway 32.

Since runways 28L and 32 shared a common section of concrete, it was incumbent upon me to ensure that only one airplane at a time arrived at the intersection. As I was vectoring the 727 to follow the A-7s, the flight of fighters passed a thousand feet below but just in front of the 727. As it did, I pointed out the traffic to the 727 pilot as little more than a point of interest. Although my original intention was to continue to provide the 727 pilot with flight directions until the A-7s were well out of the way, the pilot responded to my traffic information with, "I have the traffic and can keep it in sight."

I in turn answered, "Roger, maintain visual separation from the A-7s. They're number one for an overhead approach for two eight left. Follow them. You're cleared for a visual approach to runway three two."

As soon as the USAir captain turned his airplane toward the airport, I was reasonably certain he would have trouble slowing down enough to allow the fighters to land first. But having witnessed some incredible feats by professional pilots, instead of questioning his judgment, I reiterated my previous advisory, confirmed that he still had all four A-7s in sight, and further advised him that he could widen his flight path as necessary to follow the traffic.

After exchanging farewell pleasantries with him, I sat back to watch the rest of the show on radar. As the 727 moved closer and closer to the airport without taking any action to avoid a conflict with the last A-7, concern began to replace my complacency. I called the tower controller on whose frequency the 727 captain was now talking and asked him to once again confirm that the pilot had the traffic in sight. He did and the pilot did.

Finally, a mile south of the airport, the radar targets of the two planes merged to form one single dot. In a state beyond mild panic, I again called the tower controller to find out what was going on. At the same moment I heard the voice of the 727 captain say, "This isn't going to work, I'm going around."

The pilot then circled back around to the airport and landed without any additional difficulty. Upset with the idea that what should have been a routine pattern for landing had instead almost turned into an aluminum shower of major proportions, I asked the manager in the radar room to have the pilot call and explain what had happened. At the moment, I felt that if he wanted to kill himself, next time I wanted it to happen on someone else's frequency.

Evidently I was not the only person watching or listening who thought the whole affair wasn't quite kosher. Within minutes, almost every TV and radio station in the city of Pittsburgh was calling the tower to get more information on the near–midair collision at the airport. I found myself behind closed doors explaining my side of the story to Pete, our tower chief.

In what seemed like an urgent effort to put as much distance between his policies and my actions, Pete's first comment to me was, "That wasn't a very good operation. I don't like it at all."

I was initially stunned by his hostility, but my emotions quickly turned from surprise to anger. How, I wondered, could a man who hadn't worked live traffic in twenty years and whose visits to the radar room were most frequently confined to the supervisor's desk in the back of that room so confidently pass judgment without even listening to the tapes of my conversations with the pilots involved?

For the next fifteen minutes, I listened as Pete continued to build his case for noncomplicity after the fact. If my name was about to be added to the book of infamous controllers, Pete was making it very clear he wasn't planning to join me. Only after the USAir captain who was the cause of our meeting called and confirmed that he had never lost sight of the A-7 in question did Pete relent. Apparently sensing that the noose around my neck, and therefore his, had loosened considerably, he suddenly seemed willing to let the whole thing pass.

I, on the other hand, walked away from our meeting more disappointed than I had ever been before. It had taken me almost six years to see the truth, but that day I became convinced that a man I had respected for quite a while no longer deserved that respect. Angry as I was, I felt even sadder for both of us. Our relationship would never be the same again.

When the fourth supervisor position for which I competed went to a controller who had previously struggled repeatedly just to achieve journeyman status at Pittsburgh, the handwriting on the wall finally became large enough for even me to see. If I was going to stay in the FAA and wanted to remain at Pittsburgh Tower, it would most likely be as a controller.

Upon honest reflection, I knew that this had been as much my choice as anyone else's. My outspokenness, combined with my frequent lack of diplomacy, did little to endear me to those who ultimately controlled my professional future. The truth is, if the situations had been reversed and I was the one selecting a new supervisor, I'm not sure I would have picked someone like me either.

In some Freudian way I suppose my actions reflected the idea that secretly I didn't want to become a supervisor. With only rare exceptions, I had little to no respect for the majority of supervisors I had known over the years. And as each new replacement supervisor arrived at Pittsburgh, I saw nothing that convinced me to change my position.

Still, each new day brought me closer to the realization that before long I would have to make some very important decisions. I thought about something Pete had said to me several years earlier. Seeing little chance of any immediate openings for would-be supervisors at Pittsburgh, I had made a visit Pete's office to discuss bidding on a supervisor position in Hartford, Connecticut.

After a few minutes of conversation regarding the pros and cons of moving to New England and to an airport less busy than Pittsburgh, Pete made a comment that helped to solidify my decision.

He said, "Unless you really screw up, I'd say you have a very good chance of getting a supervisor's job right here in Pittsburgh."

As I thought about his comment now, I wondered. I could think of dozens of times over the last six years in which one or the other of my feet uncontrollably ended up finding its way to my mouth. At least one of those times had led me to really screw up.

As much as I might have wanted to, I couldn't change the past and I didn't seem to be able to live with the present. The only thing I could do was alter my future. After an all-to-familiar process of agonizing and painful deliberation, I made the only decision that seemed both intellectually and emotionally wise. For absolutely, positively, without question the last time, I would resign from the FAA.

Ignoring advice from several friends, instead of the customary two weeks' notice, I felt obligated to give Pete four weeks to adjust the work schedule around my pending departure. Though I had long since given up the idea that I might be indispensable, I still felt a strong sense of loyalty to the man who had given me another chance as a controller.

What followed was one of the most disheartening months of my life. First to receive my official letter of resignation was Buzz, our new deputy chief. Although I expected little more from him, during one of his rare appearances in the controllers' breakroom, he offered me a quick handshake and simple, "Good luck, I really mean that." When Robbie, an area manager with whom I thought I had shared some special moments of friendship, heard the news he looked up at me from his desk and said, "The drive finally got to you, huh?" I wanted to say something else, but in a rare moment of resignation I just said yes and walked away.

Even my exit interview with Pete was disappointingly superficial. He talked of how he was sure I would do just fine on the outside. I said I was sorry to be leaving. He said something to the effect that it was nice to have known me. I replied with something equally inane. That was it. As I walked out of Pete's office, it occurred to me that as glad as I was to be leaving Pittsburgh Tower, he was even happier to see me go.

During the next two weeks most of the controllers with whom I had worked repeatedly took the time to say I would be missed and wished me good luck in the future. Most of the supervisors and managers, however, said nothing. Instead they seemed to take great pleasure in ensuring that my last month at Pittsburgh Tower would be anything but pleasant.

Almost every radar controller in the facility preferred working in the radar room instead of the tower, and every controller in the radar room preferred working the busy arrival positions instead of the frequently more complex departure positions. It seemed more than coincidental that I continually found myself being assigned to the least-preferred positions at the least-preferred times.

With each new day, I found the pattern of the previous day being repeated. I also felt an increasing sense of alienation and hostility. It seemed that either because I was seen as a traitor deserting the team or because I could now be paid back for past transgressions without fear of future reprisals, I was being pushed out on a limb only to have it sawed off behind me.

Whatever it was, I didn't like the results. As I had found out only too graphically with the incident involving the USAir 727 and the A-7, under the best of circumstances a controller's actions are always open to question. When those circumstances and the motives behind them become less than ideal, every minute can be an exercise in stress management.

For a variety of reasons, most of which were directly related to the health, well-being, and future security of my family and me,

I walked into Pittsburgh Tower for the last time accompanied by my attorney, Pat Thomassey. On the advice of my brother, who was most of the time my attorney of record, and my wife, I had reluctantly acknowledged that I should no longer trust that my soon-to-be ex-employer would act in my best interests. I should instead now do that myself.

As Pat and I walked into Pete's office, the restrained anger quickly made me thankful that Pat had come along for the ride. Pat was slightly small in stature, but if an initial impression led an opponent to underestimate his ability, in the first few minutes of contact his attitude and demeanor soon changed that opinion. If the opposition was foolish enough to doubt his record as a highly successful attorney, that was a mistake they would most likely end up having to live with.

The reason for our meeting was to clarify in person what an earlier, specifically detailed letter from Pat evidently had failed to do. Because of what I felt were the unsafe, unhealthy, and unacceptable conditions in which I was expected to control traffic, my remaining time on the employment roster would be spent on leave.

After several heated moments during which Pete neither admitted to nor denied my allegations, we mutually resolved that each of us wanted only to put any association with the other in the past and move into the future along distinctly separate paths. Having accomplished all that I had come for, I said good-bye to Pete for the last time.

To finally and completely disassociate myself from the FAA, I had only one or two more things to accomplish. With Pat as my witness, I removed my personal belongings from my locker and returned my government-issue equipment to the secretary charged with keeping track of it. After she assured me that I owed nothing else to anyone, it was time to leave.

As Pat and I walked out into the parking lot, I felt sadness, anger, bitterness, and remorse. Most of all I felt relief as I had never felt it before. But when I looked back over my shoulder at the tallest FAA-constructed tower in the country, I also felt a terrible feeling of loss. Not only had I failed to accomplish what I wanted to do, but in a strange way we all had. Once more it seemed that power had become a replacement for ability and a substitute for understanding.

A little more than a year later, as my wife and I prepared to move our family out of Western Pennsylvania, I found myself again saying good-bye to my remaining controller friends. I had accepted a teaching position in New Hampshire at Daniel Webster College, a small but highly reputable institution that specializes in aviation, and our friends were gathering for an informal farewell dinner together.

Of the many who had promised to stay in touch with me after I left Pittsburgh, only Ken, Steve, and Charlie had kept that promise. So this night, they and I , along with our wives, met at the Iron Bridge Inn just outside of Mercer for one more evening of companionship and reminiscence. Although it had been quite a while since the eight of us had all been together, the closeness of our friendships quickly erased the effect of that separation.

Filled with laughter, good food, drink, and good talk, the evening passed by as fast as the many others we had shared together. Only in the final moments as we started saying good-bye did I realize that this one was different. As we all lingered uncomfortably, not wanting that last minute to materialize, Charlie's wife, Lorraine, broke the ice.

As she hugged me and tears started streaming down her face, she said, "You just don't know how much we miss your being at Pittsburgh. At least when you were there I didn't worry about Charlie getting into as much trouble. I knew you'd always be there to help him out. Now he's fighting most of the battles by himself."

When she spoke, the emotions I had been so tightly controlling all night long finally surfaced. Although I didn't say much, I knew exactly what Lorraine was talking about. More than once I had looked for support in a room filled with people, and more than once Charlie had been the only one there who responded. Suddenly I felt as though, if I hadn't betrayed a friend, I certainly had let him down.

No longer able to delay the end of the evening, we started to say our final good-byes. In a show of affection that was completely unexpected, formal handshakes gave way to warm, caring hugs. At first it seemed out of character that the three men I would most want with me in a barroom brawl were the same three friends saying good-bye with traces of tears in their eyes. Then I realized the thoughts and feelings behind those tears were the very reason they were my friends.

As I stood in the parking lot and quietly watched the taillights of their cars fade slowly into the darkness, my outlook changed. Instead of thinking about the past with bitterness and anger, I started remembering all the special people who had made it so worthwhile.

Driving home that night, I gave this new sensation the ultimate test of validity. If I had to do it all over again without changing anything, would I do it? A smile slowly crept over my face as I thought, Yeah, I would, in a second.

GLOSSARY

APPROACH CONTROL. Air traffic control service, usually radar control, provided to VFR and IFR aircraft within approximately a thirty-mile radius of an airport

APPROACH LIGHTS. An airport lighting system that extends beyond the approach end of a runway to provide pilots with visual alignment

ASR APPROACH. A means by which air traffic controllers provide pilots with directional guidance to align aircraft with a runway; most commonly used as an emergency procedure or for military aircraft

BRAKING ACTION. Reports given when the runway surface may be subject to conditions that are less than adequate for normal stopping conditions

CEILING. A cloud layer, measured in feet above ground level, that is classified as broken or overcast clouds

CITATION. A twin-engine business jet manufactured by Cessna Aircraft and capable of carrying six to eight passengers

CLEVELAND CENTER. The Air Route Traffic Control Center responsible for providing radar separation for IFR aircraft flying enroute between airports in a portion of the Midwest

COMANCHE. A single-engine aircraft manufactured by Piper Aircraft and capable of carrying four persons

DRAG PARACHUTE. A parachute deployed from the rear of an aircraft to provide additional wind resistance to help slow down the aircraft upon landing

ETG. Enhanced target generator, a radar display that provides computer-generated aircraft targets to assist in training new controllers

FINAL APPROACH COURSE. A flight path that is five to ten miles long and is aligned with the landing runway

FLIGHT STRIPS. Paper strips on which is written information concerning an aircraft's flight: aircraft callsign, requested altitude, time of departure, and route of flight

GENERAL AVIATION. The segment of civil aviation that includes all aircraft except large aircraft and those typically referred to as airliners

GOING DOWN THE PIPE. A colloquialism used by air traffic controllers to indicate inability to keep up with a heavy amount of air traffic

GROUND CONTROL. The control position in an air traffic control tower responsible for all movement of aircraft and vehicles on inactive runways, certain ramp areas, and taxiways

GULFSTREAM. A twin-engine turboprop aircraft manufactured by Gulfstream and capable of carrying ten to twelve passengers

HUB-AND-SPOKE. A concept by which major air carriers and their affiliated air taxi carriers bring passengers from outlying airports to a central hub airport, transfer the passengers to connecting flights, and then depart for the spoke airports

ILS. Instrument landing system, which provides electronic lateral and vertical guidance to help pilots align accurately with a landing runway in conditions of reduced visibility

IFR. Instrument flight rules, which govern flying with reference to instruments only

IFR CLEARANCE. An authorization provided by air traffic control that enables pilots to fly in clouds or in areas of reduced visibility with adequate separation of aircraft

INSTRUMENT WEATHER. Weather conditions in which pilots are unable to see outside the airplane to locate other aircraft or ground references (flying in the clouds)

KING AIR. A twin-engine turboprop aircraft manufactured by Beech Aircraft and capable of carrying six to eight people

LEFT SEAT. The cockpit seat traditionally occupied by the captain or pilot-in-command of an aircraft, as opposed to the right seat occupied by the copilot

LETTER OF AGREEMENT. An official agreement made between two air traffic control facilities for the purpose of formalizing certain air traffic procedures between the facilities

LEVEL V TOWER. The highest level of air traffic control tower facilities reserved for the nation's busiest airports

LOCAL CONTROL. The control position in an air traffic control tower responsible for all aircraft on active runways and within approximately a five-mile radius of the airport

LOCALIZER. The portion of an ILS system that provides pilots with lateral directional information related to proper alignment with a runway

MINIMUMS. The lowest ceiling and/or visibility in which a pilot on an instrument flight plan can legally descend to land at an airport during periods of poor weather

MOONEY. A single-engine aircraft manufactured by Mooney Aircraft and capable of carrying four persons

OJT INSTRUCTION. On-the-job training during which a fully trained air traffic controller provides individual instruction to a controller in training

OPERATING INITIALS. The set of initials, used for identification purposes, which an air traffic controller must use during any inter- or intra-facility communications with other controllers

PRIMARY TARGET. The actual radar energy return reflected from an aircraft as it is seen on a radarscope

RADAR HANDOFF. The means by which an air traffic controller transfers control responsibility of an aircraft to another controller

RADARSCOPE. The console and screen an air traffic controller uses to "see" aircraft through the use of radar

ROCKWELL COMMANDER. A twin-engine turboprop aircraft manufactured by Rockwell International and capable of carrying four to six passengers

SPEED CONTROL. A method of aircraft separation used by air traffic controllers in which pilots are instructed to fly at designated speeds to avoid conflict with other aircraft

TRACON. Terminal radar approach control, the room that houses the radarscopes and controllers providing radar services to pilots within the confines of approach control airspace

TRANSCEIVER. In air traffic control facilities, a battery-operated transmitter and receiver used as backup communications equipment

TRANSMITTING IN THE BLIND. Transmitting without knowing whether the persons being called can receive or have received the transmission

TRANSPONDER. The airborne radio beacon receiver that receives/ transmits to an interrogation unit on the ground, the signal of which is transformed into a large target on a radarscope

TWIN BEECH. A twin-engine aircraft manufactured by Beech Aircraft and capable of carrying four to six passengers

VFR. Visual flight rules, which govern flying with reference to what the pilot sees in the air and on the ground

VISIBILITY. The ability to see and identify prominent objects during the day or night

VOR. Very high frequency omnidirectional range, an electronic navigational aid that provides pilots with 360 degrees of course information, the network that is the primary means of instrument navigation in the United States